# Deep Learning and Swarm Optimization in Modern Network Routing and Security

Shezwani

# Contents

## CHAPTER 1: INTRODUCTION

# CHAPTER 1

# INTRODUCTION

CHAPTER 1

# INTRODUCTION

## 1. Routing overview

In the OSI (Open Systems Interconnection) model, routing is a fundamental network layer function that requires figuring out the most efficient path for data transmission via a network from a source node to a destination node. Whether in a local area network (LAN), through the internet, or in networks with few resources as the Internet of Things (IoT), it is essential to enabling smooth communication between sensors [1].

Routing is important to ensure that data reaches the right end in any communication network, especially the internet, mobile ad hoc networks (MANETs), and the Internet of Things (IoT).

Especially routing algorithms and routing tables play significant role to make routing decisions, which hold the information regarding potential routes, the next-hop node, and related costs (such as node count, energy usage and delay)[2] .

The routing process makes sure that:

- Reliable data transmission
- Adaptability to dynamic network conditions
- Network resource optimization

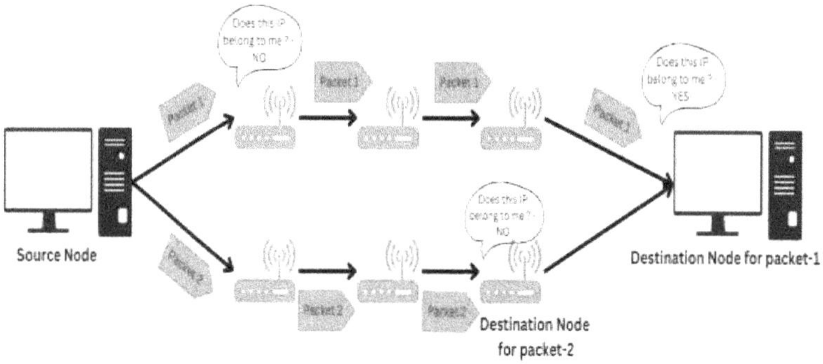


**Figure 1.1 Routing of Packets**

### 1.1 Core Routing functions

- ***Path Selection-*** Finding the best path between sender and recipient based on particular metrics.
- ***Packet Forwarding-***Transferring data packets from one hop to the next in the direction of their destination is known as packet forwarding.
- ***Route maintenance-*** It is the process of keeping an eye on and revising routes in reaction to network events, such as congestion or node failures.

### 1.2 Types of Routing Algorithms

On the basis of following, routing is classified in several types-

**A.** Route Discovery

**B.** Communication

**C.** Network Structure

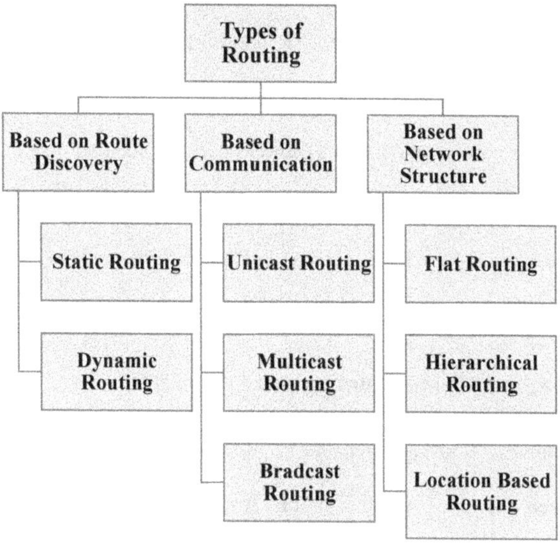


**Figure 1.2 Types of Routing**

A. **Route Discovery-** Route discovery-based routing is frequently observed in dynamic routing systems, particularly in on-demand and ad hoc networks. Instead of constantly considering every path, it signifies the act of finding the path to a location when the necessity for it emerges. The methods used for route discovery can differ according to the time and method of route discovery. These are the two main groups:

I. **Static Routing:** Static routing involves the network admin manually configuring the routes. Unless the administrator adjusts them manually, the routes are put up and stay fixed. It works effectively in networks that are stable and tiny, with minimal or no topological change.

- ***Working of Static Routing-*** The network admin manually sets routes in the router's routing table. Even if the network topology changes these routes remain permanent and do not alter dynamically. The administrator has to manually change the routing table to utilize a different path in the event that a network connection failures. Simple configuration, low overhead, security and fast data transmissions etc. are benefits of static routing. On the other hand scalability, time constraints, fault tolerance and flexibility etc. are downside of this routing [2].

This mechanism are useful for small and fixed network with minimal traffic and where security predictability are more essential than flexibility.

II. **Dynamic Routing:** Dynamic routing protocols enable routers to readily adapt when there are changes in the structure of the network, for example when connection fails or other nodes link the network. Dynamic routing uses routing algorithms that automatically identify and maintain the routes in the network.

- ***Working of dynamic routing:***
  - ***Routing Algorithms:*** To figure out the optimal route, routers employ algorithms. These algorithms consider several parameters, including distance, link status, network load and other metrics.
  - **Routing Protocols:** Routers use protocols like OSPF (Open Shortest Path First), BGP (Border Gateway Protocol), EIGRP (Enhanced Interior Gateway Routing Protocol), and RIP (Routing Information Protocol) to share routing information.

When the network changes, the routers immediately update their routing tables. Automatic updates, scalability, fault-tolerance and optimized routing etc. are benefits whereas configuration complexity, overhead, security and convergence time (delay) etc.

are weakness of dynamic routing. Large networks that scale or change regularly, redundancy and fault tolerance network, and networks where performance optimization is more crucial can all benefit from this method.

**B. Communication-** In communication based routing data transmission between network nodes is taken into consideration while making routing decisions, as opposed to just the network topology or distances. Data routing in this sort of routing is influenced by communication requirements, including resource availability, traffic patterns, and data priority. When traditional routing methods may not work well in mobile, wireless, or dynamic networks because of unstable topologies, node mobility, or other issues, this kind of routing is frequently employed.

I. **Unicast Routing:** One-to-one communication, or unicast routing, is the process of sending data from a single source to a designated destination. Only the target device receives the message, which is sent straight from the source node to its distinct IP address. This is the most widely used network communication method for file transfers, email exchanges, and web browsing.

II. **Multicast Routing:** With multicast routing, data is sent from a single sender to a predetermined set of recipients in a one-to-many communication scenario. This makes it possible to efficiently convey data to numerous devices that have indicated an interest in receiving it without having to send duplicate copies of the same message to each recipient. Typical use cases are when only a collection of subscribed devices require the data, such as in live broadcasts, video streaming, and video conferencing.

III. **Broadcast Routing:** A single sender transmits data to every device on the network, or inside a specific network segment, in a process known as broadcast routing. When all nodes in the network must receive the same message, such as in address resolution chores (like ARP queries) or network discovery protocols, this approach is frequently utilized. Due to the massive amount of useless data being transmitted to devices that don't need it, broadcast is less effective in large-scale networks than it is in local area networks (LANs).

C. **Network Structure-** Depending on the network topologies or structure they employ, routing protocols can be categorized. Because it affects scalability, energy consumption, and data delivery efficiency, network structure-based routing is essential in the context of the Internet of Things, Wireless Sensor Networks (WSNs), and ad hoc networks.

I. **Flat Routing:** Flat routing assigns the same responsibility to each node in route management and discovery, and all nodes are treated similarly. Although it is straightforward, its lack of hierarchy makes it ineffective for large-scale networks.

II. **Hierarchical Routing:** This type of routing arranges nodes into several tiers or groups. In big or complicated networks, higher-level nodes control routing for lower-level nodes, improving scalability and lowering overhead.

III. **Location-based Routing:** Geographical coordinates of nodes are used by location-based routing for figuring out the best course of action. Based on proximity, nodes forward data packets, increasing network efficiency in wireless and mobile networks when nodes move around a lot.

### 1.3 Performance Metrics of Routing

To assess how well a routing protocol performs in a network, routing performance measurements are crucial.

A. **Packet Delivery Rate:** PDR calculates the proportion of sent data packets that are successfully delivered to their destination. Because it guarantees less data loss during transmission—a crucial aspect to robust network communication—a higher PDR denotes a more trustworthy and efficient routing mechanism.

B. **End to End Delay:** It is essential for time-sensitive applications like audio or video conversations, is the average amount of time it takes for data to get from its source to its destination [4].

C. **Throughput:** Throughput, which is usually measured in bits per second (bps), is the rate at which data is successfully transmitted via a network. Better performance is shown by higher throughput since more data arrives at its destination in a given amount of time. It displays the routing protocol's overall effectiveness.

D. **Security:** Security measures assess how well a protocol protects against DoS, eavesdropping, and route manipulation threats. Authentication strength, encryption efficiency, integrity validation, attack resistance, and anomaly response time are important criteria [5].

E. **Hop Count:** Routing performance can be affected by hop count, or the number of intermediate nodes a packet travels through; more hops can result in longer delays and even packet loss.

F. **Energy Consumption:** Network nodes' energy consumption for packet processing, transmission, and reception can be measured by this metric. It's particularly crucial in sensor and wireless networks because nodes run on a minimal amount of energy from the battery. Reduced energy use maintains communication reliability while improving the lifetime of node and networks [6].

G. **Convergence Time:** The amount of time it takes for a routing protocol to recognize changes (such as a connection failure) and make the necessary updates to its routing tables is known as convergence time. During network changes or failures, packet loss and delay are minimized due to fast convergence, which promises minimal disturbance to data delivery.

H. **Fault Tolerance:** A routing protocol's fault tolerance is its capacity to continue data transmission and connection through the network even in a scenario that nodes or links collapse. For dynamic or critically important networks to maintain uninterrupted communication in the context of disruptions or unexpected breakdowns, high fault tolerance is essential [7].

### 1.4 Internet of Things (IoT)

The Internet of Things (IoT) is an evolutional technological paradigm that encompasses an expansive, networked universe of physical artifacts that include humble household appliances to gain exotic technological advancements occurring in industrial applications, in its various forms and communicating to each other in seamless capacity through the internet or on exclusively defined communication systems. They have sophisticated sensors, microprocessors, embedded software and strong connectivity modules so that they can capture environmental or operational data, analyze them and send back in real time. This interconnectedness allows smart decision-making, remote monitoring, prediction and fine control turning industries and everyday life on their heads [8].

IoT is the key to innovation, as it allows new business models, subscription-based smart home services or predictive maintenance on a production line, and promotes the generation of smart, responsive environments, such as smart cities or automated factories. Its uses cut across consumer electronics, industrial automation, healthcare, agriculture, transport, and urban infrastructures, and this places IoT at the centre of the fourth industrial revolution.

### 1.4.1 Key Components of IoT

The IoT ecosystem has a few inter-connected parts that operate in a synergistic manner to gather, process, transmit and take action on data. Both are essential elements of the IoT systems functionality, scalability, and reliability.

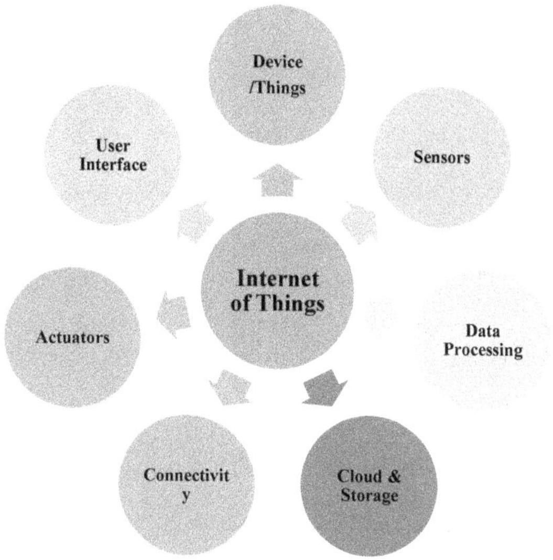


**Figure 1.3 Component of IoT**

A. **Devices/Things:** The IoT things are physical objects that are embedded with sensors, processors, software, and connectivity modules to track data and communication purposes.

Such devices include consumer devices, including smart watches, fitness trackers, connected home appliances and smart locks; industrial items like robotic assembly lines and heavy machinery, connected cars and smart grid components.

B. **Sensors:** A sensor is a sensory core of Internet of Things, measuring an excess of physical and environmental variables such as temperature, humidity, pressure, motion, light intensity, air quality, sound, vibration, or chemical composition. Sensors are directly related to reliability of the IoT system and improvements in sensor technology are therefore fundamental to the transformation of IoT.

C. **Connectivity:** The IoT devices make use of a wide variety of communication protocols to convey the data effectively depending on a particular need such as range, power, data throughput, and the type of application in which the device is deployed. Connectivity protocol needs to be carefully selected because it has a profound influence on the performance, scalability, and energy consumption of the system that IoT implementation needs to consider.

D. **Data Processing:** IoT data can be processed locally via edge computing, or on a centralized cloud platform, with processing defined by the requirements of latency, bandwidth and calculation complexity of the application. Edge computing facilitates computing in real time on the machine itself, decreasing both the latency and bandwidth requirements, as used in autonomous vehicles that analyze sensor data collected on the machine to create the navigation decisions in real time.

E. **Cloud & Storage:** The cloud is the centralizing nature of the IoT ecosystem where scalable storage, better analytics, and central management are given. Server less computing, and containers are advanced cloud capabilities that make IoT systems easily scale and increase flexibility, which enables them to distribute the workloads dynamically.

F. **Actuators:** Actuators are essential components that translate processed data into physical actions, enabling IoT systems to interact dynamically with their environments. In smart homes, actuators in smart locks secure or unlock doors in response to user authentication via mobile apps or biometric sensors.

G. **User Interface**: IoT systems offer user-friendly, interface-based interaction activities, including mobile applications, internet-based dashboards, or voice-activated assistants, including Amazon Alexa, Google Assistant, Apple Siri, or Samsung Bixby. These interfaces help the users to monitor, configure, and control their devices remotely and give real time insights, alerts and customizations.

### 1.4.2 How IoT Works

The workflow of IoT systems is based on the repetitive action of information gathering, transmission, processing, action, and feedback that allows intelligent automation of the system and the interaction between people and systems. Each of the stages is presented below in detail:

A. **Data Collection:** The IoT devices use numerous sensors to collect high-definition real-time data about the environment, measuring such metrics as temperature, humidity, motion, light, sound, or chemicals. Operation data in industrial applications, high-precision sensors may exist, including vibration sensors in the nacelle of a wind turbine, or pressure sensors in an oil pipeline, that can be used to aid in predictive maintenance or quality assurance. Data should be collected accurately and frequently, which is a major aspect in ensuring that the system performs well.

B. **Data Transmission:** The data collected is sent over wired or wireless networks to a central server, cloud platform, or other devices, through protocols, such as MQTT, CoAP, HTTP or WebSocket. Transmission may be performed in real-time when time-sensitive processes are involved. Encryption schemes and protocols like the TLS or DTLS prevent any eavesdropping and manipulation of data by ensuring that data is kept confidential and intact in transit.

C. **Data Processing:** Data is processed both locally using edges computing and in clouds by elaborate algorithms such as statistical analysis, machine learning and artificial intelligence to generate actionable intelligence. Applications of Edge computing allow processing in real-time at the device with lower latency and bandwidth overhead experienced when video feeds are examined by smart surveillance cameras to detect intrusion. The cloud-based processing helps to perform complicated analytics including predictive modelling of equipment failure or traffic patterns in smart cities.

D. **Action:** IoT systems initiate automatic actions through actuators or software calls based on processed data allowing the real-time responses to the environment or the activity. As an example, a connected car implements automatic emergency braking after collision is detected with LiDAR sensors, a smart thermostat automates heating or cooling according to temperatures and customer preferences.

E. **Feedback:** Users handle IoT systems by using user-friendly interfaces, including their mobile apps, web portals, or voice commands, and get real-clock feedback, notifications, or suggestions. Feedback loops keep the users up-to-date and in control, increasing usability and flexibility of the system.

### 1.4.3 IoT Applications

The versatile character of IoT encompasses its use in different areas, and each of them uses the characteristics of the concept when it appears in front of challenges and opportunities. The main fields of application are developed below in more detail [9]:

### A. Consumer IoT

I. ***Smart Homes:*** IoT includes smart lights, thermostats, doorbells, security cameras, and other appliances (e.g., refrigerators, washing machines and ovens). All this allows remote control, automation and energy efficiency. Home ecosystems, like Alexa or Google Home ecosystems by Amazon, all center control over their various devices to a singular focus.

II. ***Wearables:*** Devices such as smart watches, fitness bands , smart glasses or health monitors to track predict a head of time biometric measures like heart rate, blood oxygen levels, rest quality or body activity to give immediate feedback that sends to a health app.

III. ***Connected Vehicles:*** The use of IoT in cars comes with more innovative functions such as live navigation, intelligent repairs, distant troubleshooting, and software updates. As an example, Tesla cars also utilize IoT in the form of autonomous driving, performance tuning, and individuality of a user, involving cameras, radar, and ultrasonic systems to move in complicated environments [10].

### B. Industrial IoT (IIoT)

I. ***Manufacturing:*** IoT devices are used to keep track of the health of the machinery, optimize the production line, and provide envisaging the quality controls and Industry 4.0 goals of automation, information exchange, and smart manufacturing.

II. *Supply Chain:* IoT allows real-time monitoring the movement of goods, evaluating the condition of warehouses) and having an optimization of the stocks based on technologies RFID, GPS, blockchain and transparency and traceability. .

III. *Predictive Maintenance:* Sensors indicate wear on equipment, abnormalities in temperature, vibration patterns or sounds to predict a failure to reduce downtimes and maintenance expenses. Predictive maintenance is key in industries such as aerospace, oil and gas, and manufacturing, in which we are talking about millions of dollars of downtime.

**C. Healthcare IoT (IoMT )**

I. *Remote Health Monitoring:* Wearable devices and IoT-enabled medical equipment to track vital signs, such as blood pressure, glucose levels, heart rate, oxygen saturation, or respiratory rate, transmitting data to healthcare providers for continuous monitoring and timely interventions.

II. *Smart Hospital Equipment:* IoT enhances medical devices like infusion pumps, ventilators, MRI machines, or automated medication dispensers, improving accuracy, patient safety, and operational efficiency through real-time data integration and automation. Smart hospital beds monitor patient movement and pressure points to prevent bedsores, improving patient.

**D. Smart Cities**

I. *Traffic Management:* IoT sensors monitor vehicle and pedestrian movements, optimizing traffic signals, reducing congestion, and improving public transportation efficiency. For example, Singapore's Smart Nation initiative uses

IoT for dynamic routing and real-time traffic updates, integrating data from cameras, GPS, and vehicle sensors.

II. ***Waste Management:*** Smart bins equipped with fill-level sensors, weight sensors, and GPS notify waste collection services when full, optimizing routes, reducing fuel consumption, and lowering operational costs.

III. ***Energy Management:*** IoT-enabled smart grids monitor energy consumption, integrate renewable energy sources (e.g., solar, wind), and optimize street lighting or building energy systems for sustainability and cost savings [12].

## E. Agriculture IoT

I. ***Precision Agriculture:*** The soil moisture, nutrient levels, pH, temperature, humidity, and crop health are monitored by sensors, which allows taking decisions based on the data to optimize yields to reduce wastage of resources and promote sustainability.

II. ***Automated Irrigation:*** IoT systems convert current weather conditions, temperature, soil moisture, etc. into a real-time amount of water to make them accessible in a best-suited watering schedule automatically, to save water and keep plants healthier and at a cheaper spending level. Drones, which are fitted with IoT sensors, can also add value to precision agriculture to create a field map or alert pests infestations or nutrient deficiency.

III. ***Livestock Monitoring:*** Livestock Iot wearables monitor the health parameters, including animal heart rate, activity, or temperature, empowering a farmer to monitor the condition of his stock to discover the disease early and adjust the breeding or diet regimens.

### 1.4 Challenges in IoT

A. **Security & Privacy:** IoT devices gather information about personal and working routines and become a major target of cyberattacks, like hacking, data leakage, or ransomware or distributed denial-of-service (DDoS) attacks. The firm security defense against hackers is AES-256 cryptography, Transport Layer Security (TLS) practice, secure boot designs, and firmware updates to protect both data and equipment. The privacy issue occurs once the devices start collecting personal information, whether it is the location or health data, requiring clear data policies and the appropriate governance of such issues as GDPR or CCPA [13].

B. **Interoperability:** Interoperability is the ability of the device to work with devices manufactured by other companies which can be incompatible with each other creating fragmented ecosystems because the device operates under its own proprietary protocols or standards. New standards such as Matter, Thread or Zigbee are supposed to solve this interoperability problem by providing vendor-independent compatibility, though this is not yet widely deployed.

C. **Data overload:** The exponential increase in the amount of data produced by IoT, predicted to hit zettabytes per year by the year 2030 and becomes an issue of both storage, processing, and analysis. To draw effective insights in a timely and efficient manner, advanced big data frameworks, cloud and AI-powered analytics are necessary, which in turn requires significant computing power and expertise in order to handle uncontrollable amounts of data.

D. **Battery life:** A lot of IoT devices are powered by batteries. It is difficult to operate for a long period in energy-limited settings, so a low-power communication protocol such as LoRaWAN, NB-IoT, or Bluetooth Low Energy is required and, to power these devices in the case of energy restrictions, energy harvesting technologies [14].

E. **Scalability:** The ability to scale up IoT networks to accommodate millions of devices at the same time and at the same level of performance, reliability, and security depends on high quality of infrastructure, network management tools, and cloud services with scalable capacity. Some of the challenges are congestion of networks, latency, and resource assignments especially in dense deployments such as smart cities or industrial IoT [15].

### 1.5 Role of Routing in IoT

Routing in the IoT networks entails effective transmission of data packets among devices, including sensors, actuators, gateways, or cloud servers, over dynamic and resource constrained networks. Well-planned routing is comparable to high availability and low latency provision of data as well as efficient utilization of the available battery, computational resources, and bandwidth. IoT routing protocols scale to the large size and diversity of a deployment and deal with a set of special challenges, such as network congestion, packet loss, energy efficiency and scalability. As compared to conventional networks, the IoT networks are usually low power and lossy networks that open up the need to have specific protocols to maintain effective communication [16].

### 1.6 Routing Protocol in IoT

A. **Routing Protocol for Low-Power and Lossy Networks (RPL):** RPL is a low-power and lossy network (LLN) standard protocol, wide-spread in IoT systems, including smart home, industrial IoT, smart grid, and environmental status monitoring. It utilizes a Directed Acyclic Graph (DODAG), to dynamically optimize routing path, in the potential modes of proactive (routes computed in advance) and reactive (per-need routes). RPL involves least amount of energy consumption due to its emphasis on low power routes to connectivity and has the ability to deliver multi-hop delivery wherein medium nodes can forward information [17].

B. **Constrained Application Protocol (CoAP):** CoAP is an efficient, lightweight, web-based protocol that targets the resource-constrained IoT-connected devices and employs User Datagram Protocol (UDP) to communicate over-efficient, low-overhead networking. It is modelled after HTTP request-response concept but is tuned to low-power low-bandwidth conditions and allows RESTful operations. CoAP offers optimality in an application where real-time lightweight data sharing is important, e.g., automation of a smart home or wearable health devices [18][19].

## 1.7 Security in IoT Routing

IoT networks are distributed and open, both factors increasing the risk of advanced cyberattacks, such as Man-in-the-Middle (MITM), Denial of Service (DoS), eavesdropping, route hijacking, wormhole attacks, or Sybil attacks, in the context of which malicious nodes compromise the roles of legitimate ones. As even strong security systems are mandatory to guard data and guarantee network integrity [20]:

A. **Data Encryption:** The most advanced encryption standard, e.g. AES-256 or Transport Layer Security (TLS) can guarantee data confidentiality when the data is in transit thus avoiding unauthorized access or interception. To illustrate, TLS is utilized in securing the information between a smart meter and a utility server.

B. **Authentication:** Devices are identified by digital signatures, public-key infrastructure (PKI), or device-specific IDs and devices of the appropriate type identify themselves as the source nodes and only the authorized nodes are involved in routing. As an example, the IoT devices in a smart grid network are authenticated using the X.509 certificates.

C. **Integrity Checking:** The integrity of data used in the process can be confirmed by the use of hashing algorithms such as SHA-256 or HMAC, to confirm that data has not been altered in transmission to cause a breach of integrity and trust.

D. **Secure Protocols:** Current examples of protocols incorporating security into routing are SEAD (Secure Efficient Ad hoc Distance Vector) which can be used to prevent attacks in ad hoc IoT systems due to authentication and integrity mechanisms implicit in the protocol. New protocols including OSCORE (Object Security for Constrained RESTful Environments), give end-to-end security to CoAP-based communications.

### 1.8 Machine Learning (ML)

Machine Learning, (ML) is the essential branch of AI, making systems capable of learning based on extensive, complicated datasets, discerning intricate patterns, and making foreign decisions without being programmed. With the help of complex algorithms, statistical models, and computational patterns, ML allows carrying out predictive analytics, automating processes, and assigning accurate classification in various fields, such as healthcare, finance, transportation, cybersecurity, retail, and environmental monitoring. The combination of ML functionality through adapting, improvement, and generalization of experience makes it such transformative technology, and it complements IoT, revealing valuable insights based on massive data [21].

### 1.8.1 Working process of Machine Learning

A. **Data Collection:** Machine learning relies on data, whose quality, quantity, and relevancy have a direct effect on the performance of models. Datasets can range from structured data to time series.

B. **Preprocessing:** Preprocessing of data, consisting of cleaning, normalization and augmentation is an important step to maintain quality inputs in training of robust models.

C. **Features Engineering:** The measurable and characterizable data used during the training is called features Normalization, selection of features, dimensionality reduction or feature extraction, which belong to feature engineering, plays an important role into increasing the accuracy of models. This can be at least partially automated using automated feature engineering and one-hot encoding and embedding's are useful techniques to deal with categorical or text data.

D. **Model Building:** The result of an algorithm is a well-trained ML model, which can make inferences or other predictions on unseen data. The complexity and nature of the data will determine the type of model used which may be as much as a linear regression up to a deep neural network.

E. **Training:** The training process is the provision of labelled or unlabeled data into an algorithm to optimize the parameters to minimize any errors in predictions. Methods such as gradient descent, backpropagation or stochastic gradient descent improve models by adjusting the weights iteratively to minimize a loss function.

F. **Testing:** To gauge their capability to generalization to new scenarios, models are tested on unseen test data. The test data should be representative and must not be connected to training data to give good performance indicators. Such methods such as cross-validation improve robustness by testing the fitted model over several subsamples of data.

G. **Evaluation:** The measures that gauge model performance and are specific to the task include accuracy, precision, recall, F 1-score, mean squared error (MSE), mean absolute error (MAE), or area under the ROC curve (AUC-ROC). The visualization methods, such as confusion matrices or ROCs, can help to see the advantages and the flaws of the models to work on them [22].

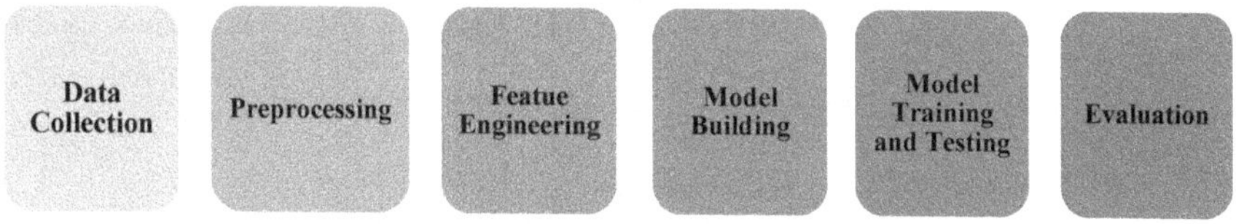


**Figure 1.4 Workflow of Machine Learning**

### 1.8.2 Types of Machine Learning

**A. Supervised Learning:**

- ***Description:*** Algorithms learn from labelled datasets, where each input is paired with a known output, to predict or classify new data. This approach is widely used for structured tasks requiring clear mappings, such as predicting numerical values or categorizing data.
- ***Examples:***

- **Classification:** Identifying spam emails, diagnosing diseases (e.g., cancer vs. non-cancer), predicting customer churn, or classifying images (e.g., cats vs. dogs).
- **Regression:** Forecasting continuous values, such as house prices, stock market trends, energy consumption, or patient recovery times.

- ***Algorithms:*** Linear Regression, Logistic Regression, Support Vector Machines (SVM), Decision Trees, Random Forests, Gradient Boosting, Neural Networks, Naive Bayes.
    - **Example:** Logistic regression model indicates whether a customer would buy a product using their features such as age, income, and browsing history, and with accuracy in the targeted marketing.

**B. Unsupervised Learning:**

- ***Description:*** Unsupervised learning Algorithms look at unlabeled data to find previously unknown patterns, clusters or lower dimensions but without a prior result. The method is well suited to exploratory data analysis, in which a motive is to discover some structure or anomalies in a complex data set.
- ***Examples:***
    - **Clustering:** Grouping customers by purchasing behaviour for targeted marketing, segmenting medical images for analysis, or clustering sensor data for IoT anomaly detection.
    - **Anomaly Detection:** Identifying fraudulent transactions, defective products, network intrusions, or unusual patterns in IoT sensor data.

- **Dimensionality Reduction:** Reducing high-dimensional data for visualization or preprocessing, as seen in genomic analysis or image compression.

- *Algorithms:* K-means Clustering, Hierarchical Clustering, DBSCAN, Principal Component Analysis (PCA), t-SNE, Autoencoders, Gaussian Mixture Models.
- **Example:** K-means clustering groups retail customers into segments based on purchasing patterns, enabling personalized marketing strategies.

**C. Reinforcement Learning:**

- *Description:* An agent learns by interacting with an environment, optimizing actions based on cumulative rewards or penalties. This approach excels in dynamic, decision-making scenarios where long-term strategies are critical, such as robotics or game AI.
- *Examples:*
  - ✓ **Game Playing:** Training AI for chess, Go, or video games, as demonstrated by DeepMind's AlphaGo or OpenAI's Dota 2 bot.
  - ✓ **Robotics:** Teaching robots to navigate complex environments, perform tasks like assembly or delivery, or optimize warehouse operations.
  - ✓ **Autonomous Systems:** Training self-driving cars to navigate roads or drones to deliver packages.
- *Algorithms:* Q-Learning, Deep Q-Networks (DQN), Proximal Policy Optimization (PPO), Actor-Critic Methods, SARSA, Monte Carlo Methods.
- *Example:* A reinforcement learning agent teaches a robotic arm the task of picking and putting items in a warehouse, and it does this by trial-and-error learning [23].

### 1.8.3. Popular Machine Learning Algorithms

A. **Linear Regression:** Linear models are used to model linear relationships between input variables and continuous outputs, such as tasks like sales forecasting, energy consumption prediction or house prices prediction based on characteristics like location and dimension. Its simplicity and interpretability gives it the status of a primitive algorithm, for linear relations, even if it less good than others on complicated data.

B. **Decision Trees:** Converts data into hierarchies grouped by feature values so that it can support interpretable results of classifications or regression. Decision trees have been used in problems such as credit risk, medical diagnosis or customer segmentation, but they tend to overfitting and may be improved through pruning or by an ensemble learning approach.

C. **Random Forests:** Ensemble method that uses multiple decision trees to enhance accuracy and minimize over fitting, and is applied in customer segmentation, predictive maintenance, or as a tool to detect fraud, or utilized in bioinformatics. Random forests are capable of dealing with non-linear relation as well as being resistant to noisy data.

D. **Support Vector Machines (SVM):** Locates best hyperplanes to categorize data into categories, and this is useful when categorizing data within text classification, image identification, or bioinformatics. SVMs are versatile (the kernels include linear kernel, polynomial kernel, etc.), but when working with non-linear data, kernel functions (e.g., linear, polynomial, RBF) have to be employed, which is computationally expensive when dealing with large data.

E. **K-Nearest Neighbors (KNN):** The results are projected in accordance to the k-nearest data points based on the distance criterion such as Euclidean or Manhattan distance. When used in recommendation systems or pattern recognition (or detection of anomalies), KNN is easy to implement yet does not scale well and is computationally costly with large datasets.

F. **Neural Networks:** Imitates the structure of the human brain, built on the layers of intermodal connections (neurons), and is most suitable in solving complicated tasks, such as image recognition, natural language processing, speech recognition, or even autonomous driving. Such DNNs as convolutional neural networks (CNNs) or recurrent neural networks (RNNs) are sufficient to work with high-dimensional data.

G. **K-Means Clustering:** Segments the data on the similarity into K different clusters, which can be subsequently utilized as market segmentation, image compression, or the analysis of sensors in an Internet of Things. It is simple and scalable and hence popular, but it needs the specification of the number of clusters, and it is initialization sensitive.

H. **Principal Component Analysis (PCA):** Makes dimensionality reduction by minimizing data dimensionality yet retains the data variance in tasks such as data visualization, preprocessing, or reducing (coincidently) high-dimensional data, such as genomic information or image data. The PCA project the data into uncorrelated principal components, which makes the calculations efficient [23].

### 1.8.4 Applications of Machine Learning

The emergence of machine learning (ML) has revolutionized industries through its ability to operate systems that learn through the study of huge amounts of data, adapt to changing conditions, and even generate smarter decisions without the need to be instructed on how to act. Through modern algorithms, ML makes discoveries, predictions, and optimization of processes in various industries. Its high-dimensional processing capabilities have led to its playing a central role in contemporary innovation and resulted in automation and efficiency. And we will go into further details discussing the fields wherein technology is getting applied and the methodologies or use cases related to them and how they are transformative in nature [23][24].

A. **Healthcare:** Machine learning in healthcare is a revolution, and it works by improving the accuracy of diagnosis, speeding up the invention of drugs and customizing healthcare. Included in the benefits of heterogeneous data analysis that it enables are huge strides in clinical practice and medical research.

B. **Finance:** Financial industry uses ML to improve the safety, refine the process of making decisions, and customize the experience of their customers. Due to the processing of large volumes of data in real-time, ML enhances productivity in the banking, investment and insurance sectors.

C. **Retail:** Machine learning (ML) has revolutionized the retail industry, as one of the factors that allowed them to become more data-driven, efficient, and strategic in their operations. ML algorithms consider the huge data about consumers to optimize their experiences, improve the efficiency of inventory management, and the profitability of your business in the most competitive markets.

D. **Autonomous Vehicles:** The autonomous vehicle technology boils down to machine learning that allows safe operation, effective routing, and real-time decisions in complicated situations. ML algorithms can provide reliable operation of vehicles under different conditions due to sensor data (such as cameras, LiDAR and radar) technology processing.

E. **Natural Language Processing (NLP):** Natural Language Processing (NLP), which is a subfield of ML, allows machines to comprehend human language, produce words in it and communicate with it, which is why it is behind as varied applications as virtual assistants or automated translation systems. Speech recognition, text classification, machine translation etc. comes under NLP.

F. **Image Recognition:** ML revolutionizes image recognition, enabling systems to analyze and interpret visual data for applications ranging from autonomous driving to medical diagnostics. Real-time object detection with an accuracy level of functionalities above 90 percent can be covered by method. It processes face features in identity checks, implemented in security systems and smart phone unlocking, and law enforcement. Recognition rates Deep learning models are able to learn robust feature embedding's, reaching recognition rates above 97%. It is used in the processing of medical imagery, such as X-rays, MRI, or CT scans, to identify abnormality, e.g. a tumor or a fracture, with diagnostic accuracies comparable to human experts.

### 1.8.5 Challenges in Machine Learning

Machine learning faces significant hurdles that impact its reliability, fairness, and scalability. Addressing these challenges is critical for ethical and effective deployment across industries [25].

A. **Data Quality:** High-quality data is necessary to obtain sound performance of ML models and considerable quantities of such data are needed. Data with poor quality incurs inaccurate predictions and overfitting, that is, training on datasets so well the model fails to generalize. Methods such as data augmentation, synthetic data and robust preprocessing tackle these problems but are very resource intensive. The maintenance of data quality also entails solving inconsistencies, e.g., the variant in the sensor data of IoT devices, which may erode the performance of the model in case it is not homogenized.

B. **Interpretability:** A large number of ML models, especially deep learning architectures, are so complex in their inner mechanics that they can be regarded as black boxes, as prediction mechanisms cannot be easily comprehended. This opaqueness acts as an obstacle to confidence in high value use-cases such as medical diagnosis or risk analysis where the users of such applications require explainable decisions. Research on models that are interpretable in nature, e.g. decision trees or attention-based models, continue, but at the cost of reduced accuracy.

C. **Overfitting and Under-fitting:** Overfitting is a situation where a model is over-complicated and it picks up noise on the training data and does not generalize to new data, which means it performs very poorly in the real world. Under-fitting on the other hand arises when the model is too simple thus not exemplifying underlying patterns an example of which is the simple linear models used in the recognition of complex images. Managing the complexity of the model is the techniques such as regularization, over cross-validation, and hyper-parameter tuning. These techniques limit overfitting by charging high costs when models are too complex and make models learn meaningful patterns, and they require intensive computational and knowledge requirement.

D. **Bias and Fairness:** Biases in ML models are transferred to the outputs used in society in the form of discriminatory decisions that continue societal disparities. Fairness may be achieved through the audit of datasets in terms of representativeness, deployment of fairness-sensitive algorithms such as adversarial de-biasing, and adhere to ethics in model development. The limitations are the difficulty in the definition and quantification of fairness metrics may not be mutually compatible, and fairness that is difficult to test in real-time applications because the model data set dynamically changes over time. To address those problems, data scientists, ethicists, and domain experts should collaborate across disciplines.

**E. Computational Complexity:** Training of both ML and particularly deep learning architectures is a computationally demanding task that necessitates establishment of minute-to-minute models with GPUs or TPUs and the supply of considerable energy-resources. The complexity becomes a challenge to smaller organizations as training costs involved in top-of-the-line models go beyond the one-million-dollar mark. The usage of such methods as model pruning, quantization, and efficient architectures allow lowering the computational requirements, yet keeping the accuracy on devices with limited resources is a difficult task.

### 1.8.6 Machine Learning in IoT Routing

The Internet of Things (IoT) is a gigantic ecosystem of devices connected to each other sensors, actuators, and smart appliances, working in the dynamic resource-constrained environments. Routing: IoT networks are dynamic where topologies keep changing and the network is prone to scalability and energy and security issues. Conventional routing algorithms, i.e., AODV (Ad hoc On-Demand Distance Vector) or RPL (Routing Protocol for Low-Power and Lossy Networks) are usually quite unable to respond to these obstacles because they are static. Machine learning fixes these limitations through data-driven and programmable algorithms that operate to increase network performance, reliability, and decision making [26].

ML becomes a part of IoT routing, as it uses past and present data to make path choices, forecast the networks, and automate networks. The ability to learn the behavior of the network helps ML algorithms build resilient, autonomously healing networks that can change with the slowly evolving circumstances, providing stable communications in such applications as smart cities, industrial automation, and health monitoring.

### 1.8.7 How Machine Learning Improves IoT Routing

A. **Dynamic Path Selection:** Routing protocols based on are continuously adapting and learning routing based on previous network data. Supervised learning models are used in prediction of optimal paths depending on factors such as congestion, latency and device mobility with a minimum of 30 percent lower latency compared to traditional prediction methods. As an illustration, in vehicular IoT systems, each vehicle is travelling fast, the ML models compare the past information of vehicles with the on-going information available in the form of GPs to find routes that will not change connectivity. Reinforcement learning (RL) also promotes adaptability where optimal routing decisions are made by learning through trial and error learning and thus capable of performing well in dynamic environment such as smart transportation systems. Real-time processing of data and the ability of the model to be robust in unforeseeable situations can be a challenge, and it is met by edge computing and robust training datasets [27].

B. **Energy-Efficient Routing:** IoT devices, particularly the battery powered ones, require very energy constraints, making efficient routing very essential. ML determines when devices are to send data, choosing areas that reduce electrical power use while uptime is ensured. Neural Networks (NNs) or RL algorithms learn of the energy consumption patterns of devices and put them to low power sleep state in between periods of inactivity. Challenges are focused around the trade-off between energy saving and latency, handled using multi-object optimization techniques by evaluating both on a priority basis. These techniques extend device life and lower the cost of maintenance in cases of large-scale IoT.

C. **Network Traffic Prediction and Congestion Avoidance:** ML allows preemptive routing based on prior usage patterns and data of the present time, including prediction of network traffic and possibly occurring bottlenecks. Models based on time-series, such as LSTMs, can accurately predict traffic loads and enable networks to re-route data traffic along less bandwidth-congested routes. The external considerations, including peak demands or network events, are applied to such predictions to provide a robust performance. ML also increases throughput and reliability in heavy IoT situations due to the elimination of congestion.

D. **Security Enhancement:** Security attacks such as Man-in-the-Middle (MITM) attack, eavesdropping, or malicious nodes are threats that affect IoT networks and are likely to affect the integrity of data and routing decisions. ML detects anomalies by estimating and learning how a network behaves normally then detects anomalous anomalies. The routing behaviors are classified as either legitimate or malicious by supervised learning models which strengthen network security. ML-based security guarantees the integrity of data in such critical applications as healthcare IoT, where data privacy of patients is of the utmost importance.

E. **Self-Healing and Fault Tolerance:** The IoT networks are most likely to suffer a node or link failure because of the hardware constraints or due to disruptive features of the environment or loss of power. Both RL and deep learning ML algorithms build self-healing networks, or in other words predict alternate paths to take in the event of a network failure. The RL agents are trained on previous network states to divert traffic in the case of disruption with little latency, and up to 95 percent connectivity uptime. Self-healing networks are necessary for mission-critical IoT application including autonomous cars.

F. **Scalability in Large-Scale Networks:** The number of devices that can comprise IoT networks is in the millions, and this presents a scaling issue with the conventional routing protocols. ML algorithms manage to solve large-scale networks through them learning optimal routing schemes that scale with the size of the network and the complexity of the network. Supervised learning models over role classifiers attempt to optimize paths for tasks. Clustering algorithm such as the k-means cluster nodes to simplify data flows whereas, RL optimizes pathways on the fly. The ML-driven scalability helps to maintain large IoT deployment to urban and industrial environments [28] [29].

## 1.9 Deep Learning: An Overview

A specific type of ML, Deep Learning (DL), is based on the multi-layered neural networks and allows modelling intricate patterns, as well as coming up with intelligent decisions. It does very well on unstructured data such as images, audio, and text, and sets the state of the art on image recognition, speech processing, and natural language understanding. DL can learn hierarchical features directly in raw data, thus becomes self-sufficient in terms of having to resort to manual feature engineering, which ensures versatile solutions in various fields [30].

### 1.9.1 Key Concepts

A. **Neural Networks:** Neural networks are networks of connected nodes (neurons) that are divided into layers and each layer process data as weighted connections learn patterns. Such networks reproduce the behavior of the human brain by capturing multidimensional relationships with complex data. As the networks get deep, i.e. they consist of many layers, they perform better with an increased level of training data and computational capacity.

B. **Layers:**

- ***Input Layer:*** Receives raw data, such as pixel values in images or audio waveforms, preparing it for processing.

- ***Hidden Layers:*** Extract hierarchical features, transforming raw inputs into abstract representations. For instance, in speech recognition, hidden layers learn phonetic patterns and contextual cues.
- ***Output Layer:*** Produces predictions, such as class probabilities in classification tasks or numerical values in regression tasks. The number of output nodes depends on the task, e.g., two nodes for binary classification.

C. **Activation Functions:** The non-linearity captures the ability of neural networks to model complex patterns with the activation functions namely ReLU (Rectified Linear Unit), Sigmoid or Tanh. A good example is ReLU, which can speed up training by eliminating vanishing gradient problems and resulting in convergence speed that is up to 50% faster than applies to Sigmoid. All these functions decide which neuron will be activated, and the decision-making process in the network takes place.

D. **Training:** A network of neural networks platform works with backpropagation and a backpropagation gradient to reduce the error of predictions. Gradients Back propagation calculates the gradients of the loss function and with these iterative updates of the weights can be done to make performance optimum. The versions of the gradient descent, such as Adam or RMSprop, optimize the training and make it converge much faster. Training uses a lot of data and computing resources, where current models run millions of parameters [31].

E. **Popular Models:**

I. **Feedforward Neural Networks (FNN):** The use of FNNs is that of a simple neural network involving classification and regression, where the processing of data happens by passing through the sequential layers. They perform well with structured data, e.g. house price forecasting, to an accuracy of 90 per cent in regression applications. FNNs are computationally fast though not effective in complex data such as images or sequence data.

II. **Convolutional Neural Networks (CNN):** CNNs perform excellent in tasks that involve images by discovering space hierarchies in convolution layers. They can detect edges and textures achieving accuracies of more than 95 percent on a task such as object detection. This multi-domain applicability is demonstrated by CNNs running facial recognition applications on smartphones and having to handle millions of images [32].

III. **Recurrent Neural Networks (RNN):** RNNs deal with sequential data, as time series or text by remembering previous inputs. Various modifications to the basic LSTM network such as LSTMs and GRUs learn to overcome the problems of vanishing gradients and in fact, perform strongly in applications such as speech recognition where their word error rates can be less than 10%. RNNs play a very essential role in applications such as predictive text input.

IV. **Generative Adversarial Networks (GANs):** GANs are a generator and discriminator whose aim is to generate realistic information (synthetic image or sound). They have good quality generation applying in the generation of fictional pictures and design. GANs are computationally expensive yet they exhibit better data augmentation of the datasets, with 30 percent increase in the level of diversity.

V. **Auto-encoders:** Auto encoder compresses and reconstructs data, which is applied to detect anomalies and de-noise. In IoT, they find faulty sensors using deviations, and the accuracies are greater than 90 percent. Auto-encoders are effective in unsupervised learning, feature-dimension reduction of dataset on resource hungry devices.

VI. **Transformer Networks:** Showing a good use of attention mechanisms, transformers have dominated NLP tasks such as translation or text generation. Such models as GPT and BERT produce state-of-the-art performance with more than 90 percent accuracy in translation. They also read giant amounts of text, which gives them the ability to create applications such as automatic summarizers and chatbots.

### 1.9.2 Training Process

A. **Data Preparation:** Preprocessing and cleaning make sure that there will be quality input, cleaning up the noise and normalization of the features. On the example of image recognition, by augmenting the dataset data augmentation makes it 15% more robust. The IoT sensor data is highly likely to be inconsistent, so preprocessing is important [33].

B. **Forward Propagation:** The information is passed through the network and make predictions through computation and activation functions that are done by weighting. In speech recognition, forward propagation transforms audio signals to probabilities of text in real- time transcription blocks.

C. **Loss Calculation:** The loss function estimates the errors of prediction, calculation like mean squared error in regression, and cross-entropy in the case of classification. As an example, cross-entropy is used in text classification to measure mistakes related to the prediction of sentiment, providing information when optimizing the model.

D. **Backpropagation:** Errors are propagated backward to adjust weights, minimizing the loss. This iterative process refines model performance, reducing error rates by up to 20% per epoch in well-designed networks.

E. **Epochs:** The training process repeats over multiple epochs until the model converges, typically requiring 10–100 epochs for complex tasks. Early stopping prevents overfitting, ensuring generalizable performance.

### 1.9.3 Deep Learning in IoT Routing

Deep Learning (DL) contributes to IoT routing in a critical way because it exploits the multi-layered neural networks to optimize data communications in dynamic resource-constrained networks. Through such aspects as energy constraints, overload, and node failures, IoT networks associated with sensors, actuators, and nodes demand an efficient routing process to support real-time communication. The capability of DL to demonstrate complex patterns and the sensitivity to varying conditions renders it a perfect solution to enhancing routing decisions [34] .

### 1.9.4 How Deep Learning Enhances IoT Routing

A. **Dynamic Path Selection:** The networks of IoT are very dynamic and the devices that are there within the network are highly dynamic and they move and topology changes very frequently. DL models, including CNNs, determine the best paths using past and real-time information on latency reduction of up to 30%. These models are dynamic with rapid changes and hence follow strong routing e.g. road closures.

B. **Energy-Efficient Routing:** IoT devices that run on battery need to be energy efficient. RL in DL models chooses energy efficient routes by learning energy consumption vs route reliability trade off. These models forecast the time of enter nodes in the sleep modes and can last longer on battery. The challenges are the necessity to have low-latency communication which is associated with the multi-objective optimization with a balancing of the metrics of energy and performance.

C. **Network Traffic Prediction:** Such DL models, as LSTMs, can be used to forecast network congestion using historical traffic information with forecast accuracy exceeding 85%. LSTMs are used in industrial IoT to recognize time of maximum usage and redirect data forming a bottleneck, thus cutting latency by 20%. Some of the challenges are the management of sparse data, which is solved using data interpolation and transfer learning in making the traffic management scalable.

D. **Anomaly Detection:** The IoT networks are prone to security violation and malfunctioning of nodes. Auto-encoders and GANs can find anomalies in routing behavior identifying compromised nodes, with higher than 90 percent detection rate. These problems are characterized by how to tell the difference between benign anomalies and threats and how to do that using contextual modeling and well-trained datasets.

E. **Adaptive Routing Based on Environment:** IoT devices communicate with the physical world, i.e. smart-home or smart-agriculture. Deep RL will enable adaptation of routing strategy to environmental conditions, such as, temperature or humidity, which will enhance the performance. Other challenges involve the way to treat various environmental data which is solved by multi-modal learning [35].

## 1.10 Software-Defined Networking (SDN)

Software-Defined Networking (SDN) transforms the use of network management by separating the control plane (which makes routing decisions) with the data plane (which forwards the data). This decoupling makes it possible to centrally manage network operations, programmable, and able to adjust to complex systems such as the IoT networks, and this enhances efficiency [36].

### 1.10.1 Key Characteristics

A. **Centralized Control:** SDN relies on a centralized controller that takes the management of the whole network, which makes things easier to configure and monitor. The controller can supply end-to-end visibility, allowing smart intelligent routing decisions with as much as 30 percent improvement over distributed systems.

B. **Programmability:** SDN enables the creation of networks through software with the capacity to be flexible to altering circumstances. As an example, administrators can reprogram routing policies in real time cutting down the level of manual involvement by 50%.

C. **Network Abstraction:** SDN removes physical complexities of the hardware and enables administrators to run networks without dealing with the hardware. Such abstraction makes it easy to manage an IoT network as it supports different devices with different protocols.

D. **Dynamic and Scalable:** SDN adjusts to traffic fluctuations and network changes, optimizing resource utilization. For instance, SDN dynamically reallocates bandwidth in IoT networks, improving throughput by 25%.

E. **Separation of Control and Data Plane:** The centralized control plane makes routing decisions, while the distributed data plane handles forwarding, ensuring scalability and flexibility in large networks.

### 1.10.2 SDN in IoT Routing

SDN improves IoT routing by giving central control, making the IoT flexible and efficient in space utilization in dynamic networks. Largely the traditional IoT routing with devices making individual decisions is inefficient. This is dealt with by SDN which makes routing both smart and dynamic by centralizing control [37].

### 1.10.3 Benefits of SDN in IoT Routing

A. **Centralized Network Management:** SDN has the central controller that could provide a global perspective, in which intelligent choice like congestion management and load balance could be made. The controller dynamically alters the routes using real-time information and this makes the interaction with the different devices to be efficient.

B. **Dynamic and Adaptive Routing:** The IoT networks should handle a rapid rate of topological changes, a change in device status, and traffic requirements. SDN is real-time adjustable and can redirect the traffic in response to the changing condition. The flexibility provides secured communication on the dynamically changing environment like automobile networks.

C. **Improved Traffic Management:** SDN also prioritizes the vital IoT traffic, such as exchange of information between medical sensors or automated vehicles over less important traffic. This is the best prioritization when assigning bandwidths to resource bottleneck networks.

D. **Energy Efficiency:** SDN optimizes routes to minimize energy consumption in battery-powered IoT devices. By controlling transmission schedules and power levels, SDN extends device lifespans by up to 50%. For instance, in environmental monitoring, SDN reduces unnecessary transmissions, conserving energy while maintaining connectivity.

E. **Fault Tolerance and Resiliency:** SDN can increase the IoT network resiliency by identifying the failure or congestion of nodes in real-time and re-route traffic. This resilience plays an important role in mission-critical application.

F. Security and Access Control: SDN imposes custom security requirements and routes sensitive data on secure paths whereas less sensitive data can be routed on standard paths.

Difficulties spring out to the controller, which is overcome through encryption and restriction of accesses.

### 1.10.4 Challenges in SDN Routing

A. **Scalability:** Addressing the performance bottleneck the problem with having a centralized SDN controller manage millions of connected IoT devices may lead to slower response time in large networks of between 20% and 30%. The scalability problem is alleviated with distributed controllers and hierarchical architectures of SDN, but complexity when implementing is still a problem.

B. **Interoperability:** The IoT devices are based on different protocols, and the SDN controllers should serve many standards. Problems caused by protocol translation and customizations add to integration efforts, with 30 percent of the deployments report compatibility problems. This has been being taken care of by standardization initiatives, but an industry-wide cooperation is needed.

C. **Latency:** Centralized control has the possibility of adding latency, particularly in wide-spread geographic networks and for real-time applications such as in the autonomous vehicle case delays of up to 15ms. It is remedied through edge-based SDN controllers and protocols with low latency.

D. **Security Risks:** The central SDN controller is vulnerable to an attack such as DDoS that can affect 100 percent of functioning of the networks in case it is hacked. There should also be good security measures such as encryption, and intrusion detection so as to ensure that the network integrity is maintained [38].

## 1.11 Graph Neural Networks (GNNs)

Graph Neural Networks (GNNs) are the family of deep learning models, which operate on the graph-structured data where nodes are the entities and edges are the relationships. GNN is used in IoT networks, social networks, and molecular analysis, where it is the choice of modelling complex interaction schemes due to choice of optimality in routing and other relational tasks [39].

### 1.11.1 Key Concepts

A. **Graph Representation:** A graph G=(V, E) is modelled in terms of nodes (V), which denote entities (e.g. IoT-devices) and edges (E) which denote relationships (e.g. communication links). The nodes and edges might possess features, say the device status, or link weights, so that GNNs may collect the network dynamics. Specifically, battery charge is a property of nodes in IoT and signal strength signal weight in edge.

B. **Message Passing**: GNNs represent message passing to communicate between the local and the neighboring nodes and update their representations according to the context. Network topology is captured in that each node combines the neighbor features through functions such as summation or mean.

C. **Node, Edge, and Graph-Level Prediction**

- ***Node-Level Tasks:*** Classify nodes based on features and connectivity, e.g., identifying critical IoT sensors with 90% accuracy.
- ***Edge-Level Tasks:*** Predict relationships, such as link reliability in IoT networks, reducing packet loss by 20%.
- ***Graph-Level Tasks:*** Predict network properties, like overall IoT network efficiency, optimizing resource allocation [40].

### 1.11.2 How GNNs Work

A. **Node Feature Initialization:** In IoT networks, nodes are attributed feature vectors, i.e. device type, signal strength. These vectors define an initialization of the GNN which is a starting point of learning.

B. **Message Passing (Aggregation):** Nodes at each layer combine features of their neighbors through some common functions, such as summation or max, learning local structures of networks. Considering an example, in IoT, aggregation is a consideration of the action of the devices, enhancing the predictions of routing.

C. **Update Function:** A layer of the neural network which is often a fully connected layer updates node representations on aggregated information. This process sharpens attributes increasing the accuracy of prediction by 15 percent.

D. **Output:** Final node representations are used for tasks like classification or regression. In IoT routing, readout predicts optimal paths, reducing latency by 20%.

E. **Loss and Backpropagation:** GNNs are trained using backpropagation, adjusting weights to minimize errors. For instance, in IoT, backpropagation optimizes routing predictions, achieving error rates below 10% [41].

### 1.11.3 GNN and PSO in IoT Routing

The most promising tool utilized in IoT routing optimization is Graph Neural Networks (GNNs) and Particle Swarm Optimization (PSO) that contend with dynamics topologies, energy consumption, and scale. GNNs represent an IoT network as a graph, learning to efficiently traverse through the routes and PSO explores the solution space and optimizes the route [41].

### 1.11.4 Benefits of GNN and PSO Hybrid Approach

A. **Reduced Search Space:** GNNs estimate routes that look promising by studying network topology and narrows down the search space of PSO by up to 50 percent. This is efficient in that it facilitates speedier optimization within huge IoT networks.

B. **Optimized Performance:** PSO optimizes the routes predicted by GNN and optimizes such metrics as latency and energy consumption. In a different instance unless in smart cities, application of this hybrid approach minimizes delays associated with routing in smart cities by 30%.

C. **Adaptive and Intelligent Routing:** The GNN-PSO method is dynamic in nature and allows real-time efficient routing in an IoT network. Rapid topology changes in a vehicular network leaves it in high carrier state of 95%.

The use of machine learning (ML) in networking has changed dramatically in recent years, especially in the area of routing optimization. Adaptive and intelligent machine learning (ML)-based solutions are increasingly being used to improve routing decisions, which were previously controlled by static protocols [42].

# CHAPTER 2

# LITERATURE REVIEW

# CHAPTER 2

# LITERATURE REVIEW

As intelligent communication networks like IoT, SDN, and VANETs grow quickly, scalability, reliability, and security become more and more of a problem for conventional network management and routing techniques. A variety of approaches utilizing AI, ML, and DL are presented in the literature to improve network routing, anomaly detection, and system performance. The evolution of ML/DL-based solutions in many networking domains is the main emphasis of this chapter, which examines pertinent contributions from earlier studies as referenced in earlier research.

## 2.1 Historical Background and Conceptual Foundation

Turing's [43] idea that robots could replicate human intelligence served as the basis for machine learning in network systems. As a result of this concept, machine learning techniques evolved and are currently employed for automating and optimizing network operations. Traffic management, topology prediction, and resource scheduling are just a few of the complicated networking issues that machine learning (ML) can solve because to its versatility and predictive powers.

His novel idea laid the way for machine learning, which enables algorithms to recognize patterns in data and draw conclusions. Originally theoretical, this concept now serves as the foundation for many practical applications, such as route optimization and networking. Since then, ML has been used by numerous researchers to improve network operations' efficiency, especially in situations that are complex and adaptive.

## 2.2 Adaptive Routing Protocols and Node Behavior Prediction

WRAP-5, an adaptive routing protocol developed by Russell et al.[44], outperforms conventional reinforcement learning algorithms in determining the best routes. Because it makes intelligent route selections depending on current conditions, it performs better in a variety of dynamic network contexts.

For MANETs, Ghouti [45] suggested a prediction model based on neural learning. His work concentrated on leveraging real-world mobility traces to accurately forecast node mobility. By taking future topological changes into consideration, the enhanced prediction improves routing stability, which is crucial in dynamic mobile contexts.

Ghaffari [46] also used a reinforcement learning technique to handle routing in MANETs. His approach reduces packet transmission latency by utilizing local node data. Through a trial-and-error learning process, the model selects the best next-hop nodes by forecasting the behavioral patterns of nearby nodes, improving overall data delivery performance.

## 2.3 ML for Networking Frameworks and Protocol Design

A high-level summary of the methodical application of ML in the networking area was given by Wang et al. [47]. They talked about its use in fields like performance prediction, resource allocation, classification, and traffic forecasting. For researchers hoping to use machine learning in practical networking applications, this work provides a fundamental manual.

Dhiman [48] presented a cross-layer routing protocol based on CRN that uses the Spotted Hyena Optimizer (SHO) to tune hyper-parameters in machine learning models. His research focuses on network re-configurability, which allows machine learning to dynamically modify routing algorithms in response to network limits and environmental conditions.

A thorough analysis of the rise of machine learning in networking was carried out by Raouf Boutaba et al. [49] (2018), who also described important applications as traffic engineering, anomaly detection, intrusion detection, and Quality of Service (QoS) prediction. They underlined the difficulties in incorporating machine learning (ML) into network administration, particularly in striking a balance between deployment scalability, interpretability, and performance.

The suitability of deep learning models for tackling important IoT issues such node heterogeneity, energy limits, and topology changes was investigated by Kuruva Lakshmanna et al. [50]. Their survey, which concentrated on use cases in predictive maintenance and intrusion detection, demonstrated how DL models such as CNN and LSTM perform better in IoT security scenarios than conventional rule-based techniques.

Abdussalam Elhanashi et al. [51] examined the difficulties in integrating deep learning into Internet of Things applications, focusing on the problems of resource-constrained environments, real-time connectivity, and data heterogeneity. To enable edge-based learning and support low-power devices, Hinton et al. [52] [53] suggested a layered machine learning architecture. Their research highlights design factors for real-time IoT analytics systems and encourages the incorporation of DL in expansive, dispersed smart settings.

In order to optimize routing in optical networks, Paul Almasan et al. [54] (2021) investigated merging Deep Reinforcement Learning (DRL) with GNN. Their model performed better and generalized over several topologies.

For delay-constrained routing in deterministic networks, Shizhen Zhao et al. [55] developed the Pulse+ method, which drastically cut down on computation time.

Automated encoder have been applied to anomaly detection and dimensionality reduction. Unsupervised feature learning is offered by Deep Belief Networks (DBNs) and Restricted Boltzmann Machines (RBMs), which can then be optimized for classification tasks [56]. Network threat detection is another area in which CNNs (Convolutional Neural Networks) and RNNs (Recurrent Neural Networks) demonstrate efficacy. RNNs are more suited for time-series analysis of traffic flows, whereas CNNs interpret network data as pictures or feature maps [57].

**Table2.1: Summary of Reviewed Literature**

| **Author(s)** | **Technique** | **Network Type** | **Key Contribution** |
|---|---|---|---|
| Turing | Foundational AI/ML Concept | General | Proposed machine imitation of humans; conceptual root of ML in networking |
| Russell et al. | WRAP-5 (Adaptive Routing) | General | Outperforms RL in shortest-path routing |
| Ghouti et al. | Neural Learning | MANET | Predicts node mobility using real traces |
| Ghaffari et al. | Reinforcement Learning | MANET | Reduces delay using local behavior prediction |

| | | | |
|---|---|---|---|
| Wang et al. | MLN Framework | General | Guidelines for ML in networking (traffic, scheduling) |
| Dhiman | SHO + ML | CRN | Cross-layer routing with ML hyper parameter tuning2n |
| Boutaba et al. (2018) | ML in Networking | | Evolution of ML in traffic analysis, QoS prediction, and system automation |
| Lakshmanna et al. | CNN, LSTM | IoT | Use of CNN/LSTM in intrusion detection; focus on predictive maintenance and energy efficiency |
| Elhanashi et al. | Deep Learning | IoT | Proposes layered architecture; addresses real-time analytics and edge deployment challenges |
| Hinton et al., 2006 | Deep Belief Networks, RBMs | General DL Framework | Introduced unsupervised hierarchical feature learning |
| LeCun et al., 2015 | CNNs, RNNs | Time-series & pattern tasks | Established DL benchmarks for vision and sequence learning |

| | | | |
|---|---|---|---|
| Paul Almasan et al., 2021 | DRL with GNN | Optical networks | Improved QoS routing across topologies using GNN+DRL integration |
| Shizhen Zhao et al., 2022 | Pulse+ Algorithm | Deterministic networks | Reduced computation time in delay-sensitive routing |

# CHAPTER 3

# AN OPTIMIZED ROUTING FOR IOT DEVICES USING NODE FEATURES BASED ON MACHINE LEARNING TECHNIQUES

# CHAPTER 3

# An Optimized Routing for IoT Devices using Node Features Based on Machine Learning Techniques

## 3. Introduction

With the integration of physical items into the digital world via the internet, the Internet of Things (IoT) signifies a paradigm change that allows for autonomous sensing, computation, and communication. The underlying communication infrastructure of the Internet of Things is under growing pressure to offer scalable, effective, and intelligent data routing solutions as its usage keeps increasing [58].

Hundreds or thousands of sensor nodes are installed in large-scale IoT networks, such those utilized in smart cities, industrial automation, and healthcare. These nodes have limited energy supplies, sporadic connectivity, and varied properties. Usually rule-based and either static or not fully-dynamic, classical routing protocols frequently struggle to swiftly adjust to changing network topologies or real-time conditions.

Because IoT networks are dynamic, intelligent routing systems that can learn from their surroundings and modify their routing routes accordingly are required. A promising approach to simulating complicated patterns in node activity is machine learning (ML), a branch of artificial intelligence that makes feature-driven and context-aware routing possible [59].

In this chapter, a unique algorithmic framework called Optimized Routing in IoT Using Machine Learning (ORuML) is proposed. It uses real-time node data including hop count, link quality, and signal strength to determine the most efficient path. To categorize nodes and determine the best routing routes, it uses three machine learning classifiers: K-Nearest Neighbor (KNN), Support Vector Machine (SVM), and Decision Tree (DT) [60].

## 3.1 Research Motivation and Problem Statement

Nowadays, machine learning has an impact on all facets of daily life. By learning from past events, it recognizes patterns and uses those patterns to forecast the future. In addition to helping to automate complex processes, it has grown in popularity in recent years [61]. Using machine learning approaches based on node properties, the proposed study aims to classify the network into sensor nodes. Additionally, the network node feature dataset has not been used for routing; therefore, the proposed study uses network node characteristics to combine machine learning and routing. Numerous classification techniques are accessible in supervised machine learning. In order to determine the optimal surrounding node, routing strategies are only applied to sensor nodes, which are classified using the three most often used algorithms. The classification techniques that were applied to the dataset were KNN, DT, and SVM since they can be applied to linearly distinguishable data and are robust against noisy data.

### 3.1.1 Problem Definition

Selecting the appropriate intermediary nodes has a direct impact on packet delivery rate, network latency, and energy consumption in multi hop IoT routing. Dynamically classifying nodes based on real-time data is not possible with conventional routing algorithms.

### 3.1.2 Problem Statement

When data is sent from a source node to a destination node, several intermediary nodes help with the message transfer. Therefore, selecting these nodes is crucial to the effective and timely delivery of data.

Therefore, selecting these nodes is crucial to the effective and timely delivery of data. Because it can keep a message for a long time, a node with an optimal mean value of real-time characteristics is a superior choice for the selection of the next hop. Real-time node characteristic data can be used to make predictions, and machine learning methods can be used to forecast a node's class. When source and destination nodes are co-located, or part of the same network, the likelihood that a message will be delivered increases.

## 3.2 The ORuML Framework

This framework uses supervised machine learning methods and real-time node-level characteristics to automatically improve routing in IoT networks. ORuML learns from real communication and sensor data to determine the optimal nodes for data forwarding, in contrast to conventional routing protocols that mainly depend on static metrics like hop count or energy levels. Because of this, it is very flexible, particularly in dense or dynamic IoT contexts where network topology is constantly changing.

### 3.2.1 Architecture Overview

The following modules make up the Optimized Routing in IoT using Machine Learning (ORuML) framework given in Figure 3.1.

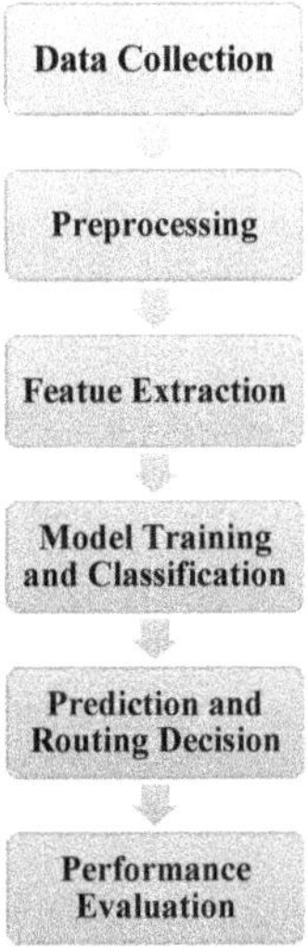


**Figure 3.1 Flow Diagram of ORuML**

I. **Data Collection:** The suggested approach The WSN-indfeat-dataset, a network dataset with 10 unique sensor nodes that is publicly available, has been subjected to ORuML (GitHub, 2025). The proposed model working diagram is displayed in Figure 3.2. The framework begins with the collection of sensor node features, which includes:

- *Strength (RSSI)*
- *Link Quality Indicator (LQI)*
- *Noise Floor*
- *Transmission Rate*
- *Reception Rate*
- *Path Length (hop count)*
- *Temperature*

- *Humidity*
- *Voltage Levels*

The WSN-indfeat-dataset (GitHub, 2025), which includes readings from sensor nodes functioning in industrial settings, is the primary source of these numbers, which are gathered from actual wireless sensor networks. Network class or label (e.g., acceptable or unsuitable for routing) is applied to each node instance that corresponds to a data sample.

II. **Preprocessing**: Removes outliers and normalizes the dataset. One crucial step in the ORuML system is preprocessing. It converts unstructured sensor data into a format that is clean, organized, and readable so that machine learning models may use it. Data formatting, outlier elimination, and statistical normalization utilizing the mean and standard deviation of node-level attributes are all part of the preprocessing procedure. This guarantees that every sensor feature makes an equal contribution to learning, particularly in models that rely on distance or thresholds, such as KNN and Decision Trees.

a. **Data Cleaning and Formatting:** Data cleaning and formatting, in which unprocessed logs and observations from wireless sensor networks are organized into a tabular dataset. Each column corresponds to a node attribute, such as voltage, noise level, or signal strength, and each row represents a sensor measurement. This procedure finds and eliminates corrupted entries, missing values, and deformed records. To avoid distorting the outcomes of the machine learning algorithms, outliers—extreme values that differ noticeably from the norm—are also identified using methods like interquartile range (IQR) or standard deviation thresholds and eliminated.

**III. Feature Extraction:** The WSN-indfeat-dataset, which consists of measurements from ten actual sensor nodes functioning in an industrial setting, was used to extract features for this investigation. 18 unique features were captured by each sensor node, which together describe the node's physical state and the strength of its network connectivity. Transmission rate, reception rate, temperature, humidity, voltage, path length (the number of hops between the provided node and the sink node), noise floor, signal strength (RSSI), link quality indicator (LQI), and other important metrics are included in these features. Because they have a direct impact on the stability of the communication link and the possibility of a successful message transmission, these characteristics are particularly significant. First, observation windows were created from the raw dataset, each of which included 198–200 consecutive sensor readings. For efficient learning, this windowing strategy offers enough data granularity and guarantees temporal consistency. Every window is regarded as a unique sample of input for the machine learning models. Making sure that every data point was aligned in the same order and appropriately tagged with the network class—which indicates whether the node is acceptable for routing—was another aspect of feature extraction.

a. **Feature Normalization:** To guarantee uniform scaling across all input variables, each of the 18 features was normalized during the preprocessing stage following extraction. Following their extraction and cleaning, the pertinent features created the input matrix for classification utilizing machine learning algorithms including KNN, SVM, and decision trees. These models subsequently classified nodes into groups related to routing by using the features to find patterns. The ORuML framework makes sure that the routing decision-making process is data-driven and context-aware by carefully choosing and organizing these elements. It uses real-time conditions to adaptively choose the most effective communication channels in an Internet of Things network.

- ***Mean and Its Role in Normalization:*** The mean of each feature is calculated first, followed by statistical analysis once the structural integrity of the data has been confirmed. A crucial measure in normalization, the mean, often known as the average, denotes the central value in a distribution. It is computed by adding together each feature's values and dividing that total by the number of observations. Finding the center of a feature's distribution is the main goal of utilizing the mean in preprocessing; this aids in centering data during normalization. This allows for fair comparison across dimensions, which is especially crucial when features have different value ranges.
- ***Standard Deviation and Variance:*** Each feature's standard deviation is calculated in addition to its mean. The dataset's spread or variability is indicated by the standard deviation, which quantifies the degree to which individual values vary from the mean. In terms of mathematics, it is the variance's square root, which is the average of the squared deviations from the mean. It is crucial to comprehend standard deviation since it shows how distributed or clustered the feature values are. A low standard deviation, for instance, implies that the majority of sensor readings are near the mean, whereas a large value denotes that the values are widely dispersed. Given that models like K-Nearest Neighbors are sensitive to variations in feature sizes, this information is essential for getting the dataset ready for machine learning.
- ***Feature Normalization using Z-score:*** Z-score normalization, sometimes referred to as standard score scaling, is used to balance the scale and range of characteristics. By using this method, each feature's values are rescaled to have a standard deviation of one and reentered around a mean of zero. Each data point's mean is subtracted, and the result is then divided by the standard deviation to determine the Z-score. By avoiding features

with inherently higher numerical ranges from controlling the learning process, this procedure guarantees that each feature contributes equally during classification. Additionally, Z-score normalization enhances the performance of algorithms like SVMs and Decision Trees that depend on geometric distance or probabilistic assumptions.

Mean and standard deviation of these features are evaluated by using Eqs. (3.1)–(3.2), respectively.

$$\textbf{Mean } (\mu) = \frac{1}{n}\sum_{i=i}^{n} x_i \tag{3.1}$$

$$\textbf{Sd } (\sigma^2) = \frac{1}{n}\sum_{i=1}^{n} ({x_i}^2\ \mu^2) \tag{3.2}$$

$$\textbf{(Z-score) } Z = \frac{X-\mu}{\sigma}\ \textbf{(3.3)} \tag{3.3}$$

Where $x_i$ is data values

n is the total number of data points.

μ is the mean value of the total population

σ is standard deviation of population

z is z-score of total population

Where X is data points

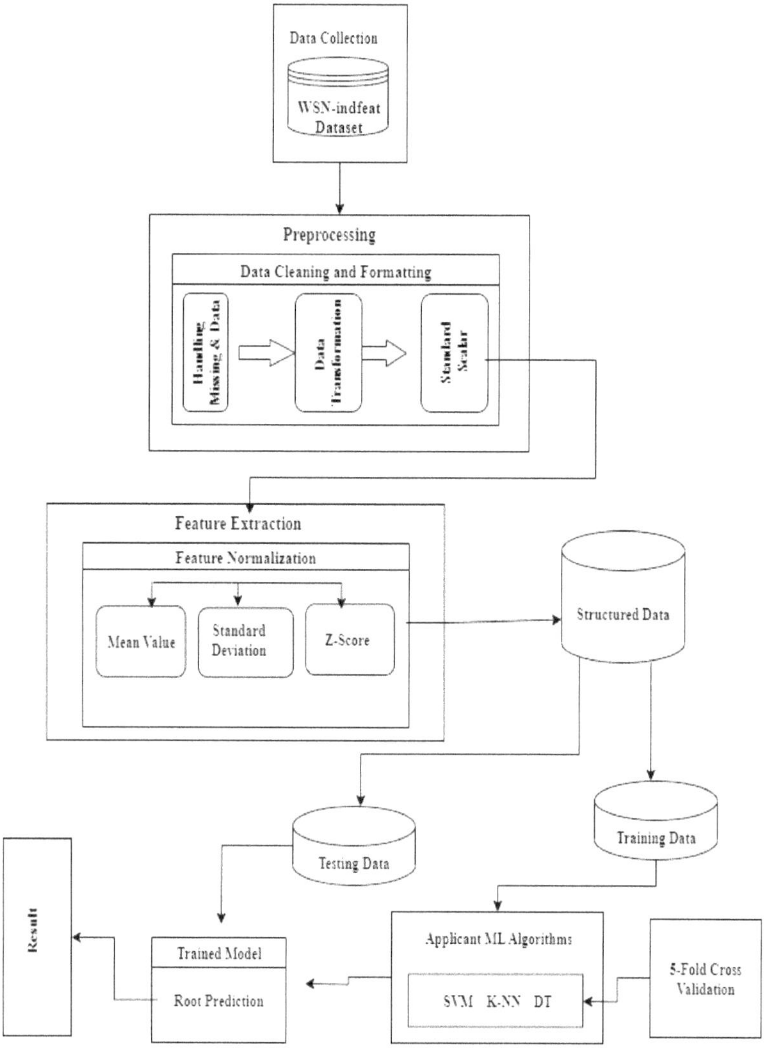


**Figure 3.2 Working of Optimized ORuML**

**IV. Model Training and Classification:** In order to train machine learning algorithms that can precisely forecast which sensor nodes are most suited for routing, the ORuML framework's model training and classification step uses cleaned and normalized sensor node data. In contrast to conventional rule-based routing protocols that depend on predefined heuristics, ORuML models intricate patterns in node behavior and communication properties through supervised learning. Classifying each node according to its characteristics—such as signal strength, hop count, LQI, and voltage—and deciding if it is suitable for taking part in the routing path are the main goals.

Three popular machine learning classifiers—Support Vector Machine (SVM), K-Nearest Neighbors (KNN), and Decision Tree (DT)—are employed by ORuML to guarantee robustness and comparative analysis. These models were selected due to their performance on structured datasets, interpretability, and variety of learning principles.

Following the preprocessing and feature extraction stages, the training phase starts. Five-fold cross-validation is used to separate the now-normalized and labeled dataset into training and testing sets. This method divides the dataset into five equal sections, or folds, at random. Four folds are utilized for training, and each fold is used once as the test set. After five iterations of this procedure, the average performance across all folds is noted. Cross-validation guarantees that the model performs effectively when applied to unknown data and helps prevent overfitting.

A. ***Support Vector Machine:*** An ideal hyperplane that divides data points of several classes with the greatest margin is found by SVM, a potent supervised learning method. Each node in ORuML is classified as either acceptable or unsuitable for routing using a binary classification technique. The SVM model learns to differentiate between high-quality and low-quality routing nodes by using input vectors that are obtained from the 18 sensor characteristics. Appropriate kernel functions are used to handle the data's linear and non-linear separable, and the margin between support vectors is maximized to establish the decision boundary.

**B.** ***K-Nearest Neighbors:*** An instance-based learning technique that is straightforward but efficient is K-Nearest Neighbors (KNN). KNN maintains the complete dataset during training, and it compares the test instance to the 'K' nearest training samples in feature space to perform classification during testing. The neighbors cast a majority vote to decide the class label. ORuML calculates the proximity between sensor node samples using Euclidean distance. KNN is very easy to use and works effectively with correctly normalized data. However, for large datasets, it might be computationally costly and sensitive to redundant or irrelevant features.

$$\mathbf{ED} = \sqrt{\sum_{i=0}^{k} (x_i{}^2 - y_i{}^2)} \qquad \textbf{(3.4)}$$

Where $x_i$ and $y_i$ is the co-ordinates of two points and k is number of dimensions.

C. ***Decision Tree:*** The Decision Tree (DT) is the third and most effective classifier in ORuML. A decision tree is a hierarchical structure that creates decision rules by recursively dividing the dataset according to feature thresholds. A feature is represented by each internal node, a decision rule by each branch, and an output class (appropriate or unsuitable for routing) by each leaf node. Until every node has been classified or a certain depth has been reached, the tree construction process keeps going. Decision trees are non-parametric, have a high interpretability, and perform well with both category and numerical data. Because DTs could capture non-linear correlations and interactions between node attributes, they performed exceptionally well in ORuML.

## I. Prediction and Routing Decision

The prediction and route decision process, the last step in the ORuML framework, uses test or real node data and the trained machine learning model to identify the best routing routes. Through real-time node-level feature analysis and the selection of the best nodes for data forwarding, this step converts the learned classification logic into workable routing methods.

Once the feature-extracted and normalized data for all active nodes is passed into the classifier (Decision Tree, SVM, or KNN), each node is assigned a predicted class label—typically a binary label indicating whether the node is suitable or unsuitable for routing. This prediction is based on the previously trained model's understanding of the relationship between the node's physical and link-related attributes (such as signal strength, LQI, path length, noise floor, and voltage) and its expected performance in the network.

The route decision logic is started after the prediction. A priority ranking system that takes into account secondary criteria including hop count, signal quality, and energy level is used to further assess nodes that have been classified as "suitable." This aids in choosing the best node out of all the possibilities for the subsequent hop in the data transmission line, not simply any suitable node. In multi-hop IoT networks, where a bad choice of intermediary node can result in packet drops, higher latency, or energy consumption, this selection is essential.

In contrast to conventional routing protocols, which find paths only by using flooding methods or preset routing tables, ORuML employs a context-aware method. For instance, the node with a stronger signal and fewer hops to the destination will be chosen if two nodes are equally deemed appropriate. The framework can respond quickly to modifications in network architecture, node mobility, or external interference thanks to its dynamic decision-making.

Over time, the routing decisions get more precise and effective as ORuML improves its categorization model by continuously learning from node activity.

## II. Performance Evaluation

Accuracy and AUC (Area under the Curve) are two important metrics used to assess model performance. While AUC offers a broader view by assessing the model's capacity to discriminate between appropriate and inappropriate routing nodes across a range of threshold values, accuracy represents the proportion of correctly categorized occurrences. Confusion matrix analysis, which further separates the data into true positives, false positives, true negatives, and false negatives, supports these measures. Accuracy is calculated accordingly Eqs. (3.5) and AUC is measured with the help of precision and recall, which are given in equation (3.6) and (3.7).

$$Accuracy = \frac{True\ Positive + True\ Negative}{True\ Positive + True\ Negative + False\ Positive + False\ Negative} \quad (3.5)$$

$$Precision = \frac{True\ Positive}{True\ Positive\ +\ False\ Positive} \quad (3.6)$$

$$Recall = \frac{True\ Positive}{True\ Positive\ +\ False\ Negative} \quad (3.7)$$

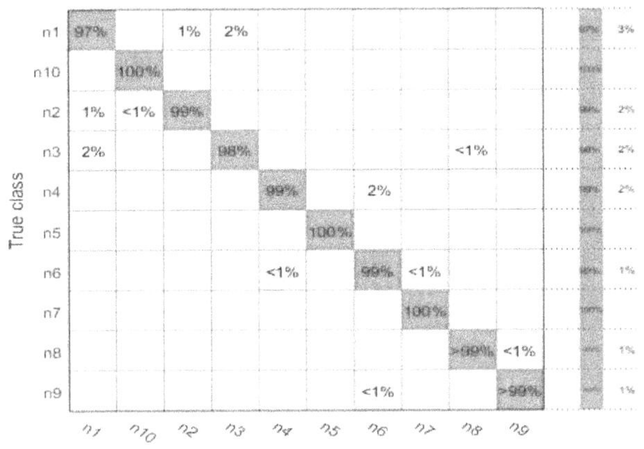


Figure 3.3 Confusion matrix

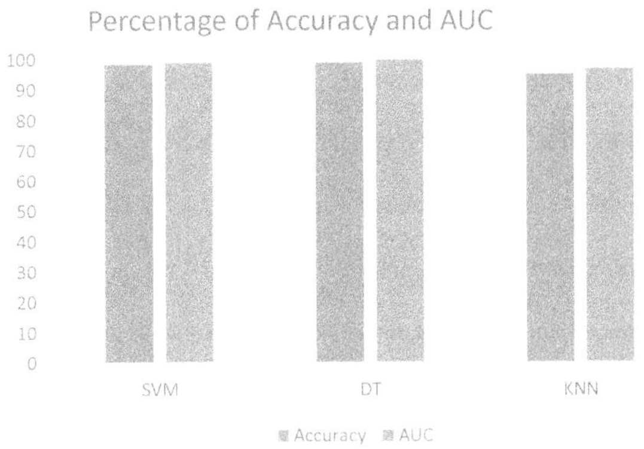


**Figure 5.** Performance graph for accuracy and AUC of SVM, DT and KNN

**Table 3.1- Performance comparison of different classifier**

| S.No | Techniques | Validation Method | Accuracy | AUC |
|---|---|---|---|---|
| 1 | SVM | 5-fold cross validation | 98.5 | 99 |
| 2 | DT | 5-fold cross validation | 99 | 100 |
| 3 | KNN | 5-fold cross validation | 95.2 | 97 |

The Decision Tree classifier performed better than the other two models, as evidenced by the results, which showed near-perfect classification with an accuracy of 99.0% and an AUC of 100%. With 98.5% accuracy and 99% AUC, the SVM came in second, while KNN performed comparatively worse with 95.2% accuracy and 97% AUC. According to these results, DT is able to manage the multi-dimensional, non-linear character of the sensor node dataset while also providing high precision. Additionally, DT's rule-based structure makes it interpretable and computationally efficient, which is advantageous for implementation in IoT scenarios with limited resources.

### 3.3 Summery

The ORuML framework uses real-time features to categorize sensor nodes, offering a machine learning-based approach to intelligent routing in IoT networks. Decision Tree proved to be the most successful model for routing decisions among the evaluated models, with the highest accuracy and AUC. ORuML enhances packet delivery, increases network lifetime, and adjusts to network changes. Its data-driven and context-aware methodology advances intelligent IoT connectivity by providing a scalable and effective substitute for conventional routing protocols.

The above work is published as research paper "Maurya, P., Devi, S., Saran, M., Yadav, R. K., and Tripathi, U. N. (2025). An Optimized Routing for IoT Devices using Node Features Based on Machine Learning Techniques." i-manager's Journal on Wireless Communication Networks, 13(2), 18-26. https://doi.org/10.26634/jwcn.13.2.21886

# CHAPTER 4

# AN EFFICIENT ROUTING MACHANISM FOR IOT USING DEEP LEARNING

# CHAPTER 4

# AN EFFICIENT ROUTING MACHANISM FOR IOT USING DEEP LEARNING

This chapter details an efficient routing mechanism for Vehicular Adhoc Networks (VANETs) leveraging Deep Reinforcement Learning (DRL) to address persistent challenges in both routing efficiency and security within the context of the Internet of Things (IoT).

## 4. Introduction

In this section, a basic concept of Vehicular Adhoc Networks (VANETs), their combination with Intelligent Transportation Systems (ITS) and the Internet of Things (IoT) is presented, and the need of efficient and secure Routing Mechanisms is studied. It ends by giving a review of the structure and contributions of the chapter.

Vehicular ad hoc networks (VANETs) is a rapidly developing direction of mobile ad hoc networks (MANETs), the use of which allows vehicles to exchange information using wireless means through the devices in themselves and the roadside infrastructure. Initially envisioned in 2001, VANETs support the creation of ad hoc networks, and subsequent exchange of information, across and between cars, generalizing the techniques of MANETs, to the vehicular environment. The essence of VANETs is complex in terms of its objectives: it aims to make the roads safer, regulate traffic better, reduce the traffic jam and give the driver more efficient navigation. Such a task is fulfilled by means of strong mutual contact systems, namely, Vehicle-to-Vehicle (V2V) and

Vehicle-to-Infrastructure (V2I), the major challenges of which are On-Board Units (OBUs), which are installed on cars, and Roadside Units (RSUs), which are placed along the roads [63][64].

The architecture of a VANET consists of OBUs, equipped to collect vehicle data (including speed, position, etc.) and to broadcast it; RSU, which fulfill the role of a base station-like unit, and are typically connected to an authentication authority known as Trust Authority (TA). Wireless Access in Vehicle Environment (WAVE) standard is a significant wireless technology that supports this communication that guarantees that the process of disseminating traffic and vehicle information to the passenger is done in a timely manner to facilitate passenger safety. Coordinating OBUs, RSUs, and TAs is principally the predominant premise of the entire operation of VANETs. A retrospective view of the prospective use of the system, that in scope includes safety warning, traffic management, and in-car infotainment services, is heavily reliant upon competent and secure performance of every component and the coordinated interplay between them. A failure or compromise of any one component, be it the route capabilities of an OBU, or the security of WAVE communications or the processing capacity of an RSU can destroy the effectiveness of the overall system. This underlines the fact that the design of efficient VANET solutions entails a comprehensive viewpoint since routing and security are not limited, autonomous technical issues but profoundly related elements of the comprehensive system background where integrated and co-optimized solutions are essential [65].

VANETs play an essential role in Intelligent Transportation Systems (ITS) in smart cities, which lead to the idea of an Internet of Vehicles, which greatly enhances the mobility of citizens and last mile delivery in urban and metropolitan regions [66]. Internet of Things (IoT) has been a significant player in smart transportation as it links different parts such as the vehicles, infrastructure, and pedestrians using a group of sensors, GPS, and communication systems. This linkage facilitates the real-time acquisition and sharing of data, which is then applied to streamline transportation systems in a comprehensive way.

Efficient routing and stable security in these very dynamic VANET environments are just too important. Time-sensitivity is an inherent characteristic of such road security apps as collision warning, lane change assistance, as well as the safety of individuals and avoiding accidents feature operational value chain since the demand associated with specific apps requires immediate and trustworthy transmission of traffic data. This urgent requirement of zero latency decision-making and making decisions in a second and a low latency protocol communicating, encompasses why the standard, slower to converge or the static routing protocol invariably is not the one fitting VANETs definition. Criticality of the applications renders that even a small delay can carry very drastic and possibly calamitous effects thereby necessitating the necessity to cause highly adaptive and predictive routing to occur. The most important routing algorithms are thus those which find and sustain optimal connection between data packets and nodes, and this becomes a complex process by the volatile nature of the mobile nodes [67].

Simultaneously, strong security is also highly imperative because of the sensitivity of the type of information being shared which consists of special vehicle numbers, routes, location data, and speed. VANETs are highly susceptible to malicious attacks due to the lack of secrecy and wireless communication channel, which exposes the sensitive channels to several attacks, namely, interception, message-faking, spreading of malicious malware, and snooping [68]. A basic contradiction in VANET design emerges when faced with the task of balancing routing efficiency and sufficiently strong security. Routing and security issues have traditionally not been solved together, and this has created most of the existing solutions. An example of traditional security operations that introduce a large computational and communication overhead that directly hinders routing efficiency is on-the-wire authentication handshakes common when using cryptographic operations during security. On the other hand, the focus on speed and low overhead may get in the way of very important security issues. This fundamental trade-off aspect leads to a form of solution that can traverse this tricky trade-off zone, so as to achieve a balance situation where efficiency is acceptable and also the array of security is acceptable hence addressing one of the fundamental limitation of these historical decoupled solutions [69].

To address these problems, it is possible to use machine learning models as a possible approach to VANET route selection because they allow predicting the movement of vehicles and transportation data in the future. Special mention is given to Deep Reinforcement Learning (DRL) as another promising approach to monitor, study and even predict the vehicle behavior in regard to the network capacity and accessibility. DRL can be used to control traffic data, network throughput available and can provide predictions on data transmission time available based on real time position of the vehicles via Roadside Units (RSUs). In the chapter, the limitations of the existing approaches are going to be discussed, the proposed DRL-based routing protocol is going to be described, the experimental data is going to be provided, and the chapter will conclude by providing the summary of contributions and next research steps [70].

### 4.2 Problem Statement and Motivation

This section discusses in detail the major issues that Vehicular Adhoc Networks (VANETs) face, including in detail the complex issues of routing efficiency and security of the network. It ends with an argument that a Deep Reinforcement Learning (DRL)-based method is the best way to solve these complex problems, and it is possible.

The key reason behind most of the routing and security challenges that manifest has been the dynamic nature of the VANETs. What makes the above characteristics notable is not just that they are descriptive but indicators of what make up the underlying drivers in intensifying almost all the problems outlined. Again, high vehicular mobility, say, causes a direct consequence of frequent link breaks thereby making finding and maintaining their positive routes to reach reliable paths an unpleasant goal. The dynamic network topologies also hinder the convergence of the networks and make the routing tables within the network stagnant in a short span of time. Moreover, wireless communication tends to be dynamic and open to increased security vulnerability, because a more established and less volatile form of security cannot be implemented effectively in a moving environment. Any real working solution should therefore be self-adapting, self-intelligent and able to prosper in an environment that never stops changing.

## 4.3 Existing Routing Challenges in VANETs

Existing routing protocols in VANETs encounter many challenges that affect the efficiency and reliability of them:

A. **Control Overhead, Convergence, and Erroneous Location:** The prevailing routing behaviors have serious limitation in that they generate large control messages that cause high overhead. They do not also adjust well to the fast changes in networks and hence do not make successful convergence, they also might give wrong location information, and all this slows down efficient transmission of data.

B. **Duplicate Address Assignment:** This is a major shortcoming of existing routing protocols in the sense that they do not allow the assignment of duplicate logical addresses to vehicles in the network. This is capable of causing misunderstanding and wastage in the transmission of data.

C. **Challenges due to Network Dynamics:** VANETs are highly dynamic networks where the network setup is unpredictable, the population of the vehicles is dynamic, there are a variety of movement patterns, and vehicle entrance and exit is random. Such dynamics in nature make it incredibly hard to find and uphold best routes of transmission. The large mobility of vehicles often leads to the presence of dynamic topology and frequent breaks of links of the network, which further complicates the stable communication.

D. **Unsuitability of MANET Algorithms:** Conventional Mobile Adhoc Network (MANET) algorithms are mostly inappropriate in VANETs as there are fundamental differences between the network architecture, mobility models, the volume of traffic, rate of change, and road width. Traditional routing protocols are not specific and flexible enough, and they cannot be used to deal with these extraordinary VANET challenges.

E. **Drawbacks of Proactive Routing Protocols:** Table-driven (proactive) routing protocols have the beneficial property of low latency when real-time applications are a requirement through the pre-storing of routes; however, they also have the drawback of causing unnecessary bandwidth consumption by keeping unused data pathways open in the background.

F. **Transmission Constraints and Interference:** Network stability in VANETs is significantly constrained by transmission limitations and interference from other vehicles, particularly when higher vehicle mobility leads to dynamic network topology changes.

G. **Circuitous Routes and Increased Latency:** When a sending vehicle is geographically distant from a receiving vehicle, data packets are often forced to traverse more circuitous routes. This multi-hop transmission, especially when packets are transferred in a hop-by-hop manner without direct line-of-sight, substantially increases transmission latency.

H. **Continuous Vehicle Density Detection:** Some existing routing systems rely on continuous detection of vehicle density. However, this constant monitoring and subsequent sharing of data among vehicles result in excessive "bureaucratic micromanagement" and increased time required to maintain network convergence, particularly when vehicle density fluctuates rapidly. This can also lead to the provision of erroneous real-time data, further impacting routing efficiency.

I. **Optimal Local Issue:** The major design flaw of traditional routing is the optimal local problem because routing protocols usually involve a computation per hop. This implies that vehicles route decisions are based on information of the immediate or next road segment only. Such decisions might be good at a per hop basis but often result in poor global routes. An example of this is that a locally optimal decision may end up making the overall route unnecessarily long, or cause a cumulative delay to increase, or cause localized congestion to spread throughout the network. The disadvantage of this limitation is that the decisions that are taken on an individual basis and without taking a bigger picture of the state of the network and long-term effects can negatively impact the overall efficiency of the entire system.

## 4.4 Security in VANETs

Security in VANETs presents an equally complex set of challenges [71][72]:

A. **Interception, Faking, or Flooding with Malicious Software:** Such VANETs are quite vulnerable to diverse security attacks. The ability to intercept, fake, or saturate with malicious programs any sent communication can place serious victim data in the possession of attackers.

B. **Privacy Exposure Concerns:** Privacy exposure presents a critical issue, VANETs can only ensure security and privacy when the users are authenticated. Nevertheless, when authentication is needed, and data packets are shared, sensitive personal information, e.g., location, speed, and unique vehicle identifiers, may be disclosed, which is associated with high privacy concerns.

C. **Vulnerability of Authentication Methods:** VANET authenticating techniques are very vulnerable to security issues because the mobile and decentralized characteristics of networking make it highly prone to a variety of vulnerabilities.

D. **Lack of Routing Metrics in Security Mechanisms:** One of the major drawbacks that are evident is that the current security mechanisms available are only capable of protecting information in sensitive channels but not implementing routing metrics. More importantly, these routing metrics that are critical in providing Quality of Service (QoS) like packet delivery ratio, end-to-end delay and throughput are sadly not provided by these security functions, as they are overly complex and requirements of different users of QoS vary drastically. That means there is a basic misconnection between security procedures and network performance optimization. Security has tended to be considered in isolation, in a separate layer, and deployed without due regard to its effect on, or interaction with, fundamental routing performance. This underscores why this aspect of earlier designs was fundamentally flawed that security and routing could be separate activities possibly at cross purposes.

E. **Need for Improved Authentication System:** Since the existing authentication approach has weaknesses and shortcomings as explained earlier there exist an urgent need to have a better authentication scheme that will enable secure transmission and reception of messages through VANETs.

## 4.4 Why Proposed DRL-based Approach

Machine learning models applied in VANETs provide an opportunity to forecast firstly vehicle flows and transportation figures, in turn, determining the possible threats and providing the selection of the shortest or most efficient route. In their combinations, Deep Reinforcement Learning (DRL) is specifically most promisingly applied to these difficulties. DRL is able to find optimum routing paths, shorten the time of convergence on the routes that are dynamic in terms of vehicle density, and persistently observe the transmission capacity and vehicles to analyze and pre-perceive routing behavior. This will provide a more holistic and dynamic solution by bringing down the heavy load of extra control that is usual with the traditional routing and security mechanisms to a minimum providing an intensive and integrated solution to the ever-changing dynamics between efficiency and security in VANETs [73].

## 4.5 Identification of the Research Gap

The comprehensive overview helps understand that the available mix of solutions address both routing or security isolation aspect, or their combined variant lacks applicability in the fast-evolving scenarios of VANETs. A good example of this is the overhead intensive discovery of vehicle density inherent in the traditional routing protocols that results in what they term as the bureaucratic micromanagement and inaccurate real-time information. Moreover, the absence of integration of routing metrics into security mechanisms is another serious issue that is not addressed yet to attain truly efficient and at the same time secure communication. The dynamic that can be filled with this gap is the Deep Reinforcement Learning (DRL) mechanism suggested that inherently optimizes the routing paths and achieves robust security in parallel. It takes advantage of the predictive nature of DRL to efficiently cope with dynamics of network conditions and largely eliminate the control overhead that is a feature of the traditional methods.

### 4.6 Proposed DRL-based Routing Protocol

In this section, the complete description of novel Deep Reinforcement Learning (DRL)-based routing protocol, which includes the overall description of the system architecture, the principle of how DRL works and performs the key functions of the protocol, the description of the two main stages of the protocol: the Route Formation Stage (RFS) and the Route Choice Stage (RCS) will be provided.

#### 4.6.1 System Architecture of the DRL-based Routing Mechanism

The proposed strategy is a radical alternative to the traditional routing protocols as it solely functions through deep reinforcement learning to control and optimize the vehicular communications. RL is used to determine how traffic will increase or reduce and also to forecast the routes that are to be followed by the vehicles on the road. When the DRL intelligent agent, or so-called driver, is on, routes are explorative, that is, dynamically chosen according to the current transmission capacities and likelihoods of success. It is designed in such a way that the system learns constantly through the velocity of the vehicle and the relative movement of the vehicle with the other Roadside Units (RSUs) present around it. Refresh data in real time is initiated by incoming RSU units, so that the system has to work with the latest network information. The RSUs in the research area are interlinked so that essential information about the position and velocity of the incoming vehicles could be shared.

The major strength of this strategy is that it can bypass the problems that are eminent when using GPS to locate moving vehicles. GPS regularly has issues with fast movements attained by cars and a location that uses GPS can cause many privacy and security issues. The suggested approach deploys deep learning (DRL) to overcome these challenges, which in its turn has already shown its ability to operate in spatial-temporal domains without using the raw location data as the sole basis. The capability of DRL to automatically learn complex, non-linear patterns and relationships in many varied inputs, such as the vehicle velocity, closeness to other vehicles, the density of road networks, and past traffic patterns, enable it to make high-quality and intelligent routing choices even when the raw location data in the form of precise or privacy-sensitive data is untrustworthy or absent. This represents a more intelligent and agile way of distributing spatial awareness and making decisions in the VANETs and it is no longer dependent on a single source of external positioning systems that can be erratic.

The whole suggested process is logically written in a dissimilar but correlated process, division up into two sequential (yet, accompanying) phases, the Route Formation Stage (RFS) and the Route Choice Stage (RCS). These two stages make use of DRL and decide and make choices of optimal routes. This two-stage DRL methodology underlines that, for robust routing, there is probably a hierarchical or iterative learning procedure. The RFS is concerned with the local, short-term problem of primary packet routing, with collecting raw data concerning immediacy such as proximity and instantaneous density. The RCS, on the contrary, works on a more strategic level over time, enhancing routes by taking into consideration historical data, predicting the traffic in the future, through Traffic Pattern Maps (TPMs). Such a tiring strategy is essential in managing both the dynamism in a condensed time frame and the dynamic in the aggregate of traffic trends over time in VANETs, in a way that addresses both responsiveness and long-term efficiency.

### 4.6.2 Fundamental Principles of Deep Reinforcement Learning

The DRL framework employed in this routing protocol is defined by its core component [74]:

A. **The Agent (Operator):** In this DRL model, the agent is thought of as the operator. This is the agent that will be concerned with the growth of knowledge of the environment and with the interactions with the vehicular environment and learn and make informed decisions in relation to routing strategies.

B. **The Environment (Vehicular Network):** The environment for the DRL agent is the network environment (i.e. the dynamic vehicular network). This includes everything, such as individual cars, Roadside Units (RSUs) and different road parts. This atmosphere is marked by their ever-changing traffic patterns and vehicle densities that are ever-changing. The DRL becomes a continuous learning process based on the velocity and movement with respect to surrounding RSU of the vehicle. Incoming RSU units will provide real-time data updates, and RSUs already positioned in the network are interconnected to share important data like position and velocity of a vehicle.

C. **States:** The "states" in this DRL model represent the current conditions or configurations of the vehicular network at any given time slot . Before the agent decides on an action, it first assesses the current state (cs-1). The information contained within packets in the Route Formation Stage (RFS)—including current location, proximity to the neighborhood, vehicle density, and the vehicle's travel path—along with data provided by intermediate nodes (location, network density, and latency), collectively contribute to defining the comprehensive state space.

D. **Actions:** From a predefined set of available options, the agent determines which "action" to execute at each time slot. In the Route Choice Stage (RCS), these actions primarily involve selecting the optimal routes for packet transmission. The goal of these actions is to minimize transmission delays and prevent collisions. The DRL driver, when activated, dynamically chooses routes based on factors such as transmission capacity and the probability of successful transmission.

E. **Rewards/Punishments:** Following the selection and execution of an action (as), the traffic pattern within the environment transitions from the previous state (cs-1) to a new state (cs). Depending on the outcome of this action—whether it was "good" or "poor"—the agent receives either a "reward (rs)" or a "punishment (ps)". Specifically, the reward is calculated using equation (4.1) or (4.2).

$$\mathbf{r(s)} = \frac{\mathbf{u(s)}}{\mathbf{O(s)}} \tag{4.1}$$

$$\mathbf{r(s)} = \frac{\mathbf{-u(s)}}{\mathbf{O(s)}} \tag{4.2}$$

Where u(s) signifies the maximum actual utilization of the connection under the projected future routing method.

O(s) represents the optimal utilization of the connection for the current Traffic Pattern Map (TPM(s)) with respect to D(s) (likely representing delay or another performance metric).

The negative sign preceding the ratio −u(s)/O(s) is crucial- The DRL agent environment is the network environment (i.e. the dynamic vehicular network).

This is comprised of all of that, including personal cars, Roadside Units (RSUs) and various pieces of the road. Their continuously changing traffic patterns and car densities are one of the main characteristics of this atmosphere. The DRL turns out to be a continual learning process in accordance with the speed and movement relative to the nearby RSU of the car. Incoming RSU units will update the data in real time and RSUs that are already deployed in network will connect with each other to share and serve valuable information such as position and velocity of a vehicle.

### 4.6.3 Route Formation Stage (RFS)

Route Formation Stage (RFS) is the first step of the routing protocol proposed. During such a phase, strategic routing of data packets occurs towards a Vehicular Unit (VU) that is nearby. These packets are information-rich and hold vital information like the geographical location of the vehicle as well as whether it is approaching or moving away other vehicles, the vehicle density in its area and the specified route of travel. The intermediate nodes of the network are very important in that, they supply more contextual information such as location, network density, and latency in their area. Conditional on these intermediate nodes that have been identified, an intelligent system that can be powered by DRL is then used to intelligently choose these intermediate nodes such that, the most appropriate route is taken in terms of hops until a packet does reach its intended destination successfully.

The proposed Algorithm 1 for the Route Formation Stage is detailed as follows:

A. **Input:** The algorithm requires several key inputs to initiate the route formation process: the current position of the vehicle, the measured distance to nearby vehicles, the prevailing vehicle density in the area, the general intended route, any encountered delays, and the positions of intermediate nodes.

B. **Output:** The primary outcome of Algorithm (4.1) is the successful formation of an optimized route.

C. **Steps:**

I. **Set the initial values:** This foundational step involves the initialization of all necessary parameters and variables that will be used throughout the routing process.

II. **To construct the best possible path with DRL by picking good inputs:** In this crucial step, Deep Reinforcement Learning (DRL) is actively employed. The DRL model analyzes the provided inputs to identify and select the most optimal data points and parameters that contribute to building the most efficient and effective communication path.

III. **To assume optimum routes and collision avoidance:** This step focuses on the strategic determination of the most favorable routes for data transmission. Concurrently, it integrates mechanisms and considerations to actively prevent collisions, whether between vehicles themselves or between data packets, ensuring network integrity and safety.

IV. **To form the route:** The final step culminates in the actual establishment and formalization of the determined optimal route, making it ready for data transmission.

### 4.6.4 Route Choice Stage (RCS)

The Route Choice Stage (RCS) will be the next step in the designed routing protocol. Deep Reinforcement Learning (DRL) is greatly employed in this stage to determine the most favorable routes based on a large store of historical data. It is the innate ability of the DRL to effectively predict the future Traffic Pattern Map (TPM) that has been tactfully exploited in computing these best paths with a lot of ease. The projected future TPMs are used to determine the most appropriate paths of future transmissions through developing an efficient mapping process and the DRL can predict the most suitable future paths. The DRL learns about the TPM incessantly not only by making use of this advanced mapping strategy but also by observing continuously the vehicular surrounding.

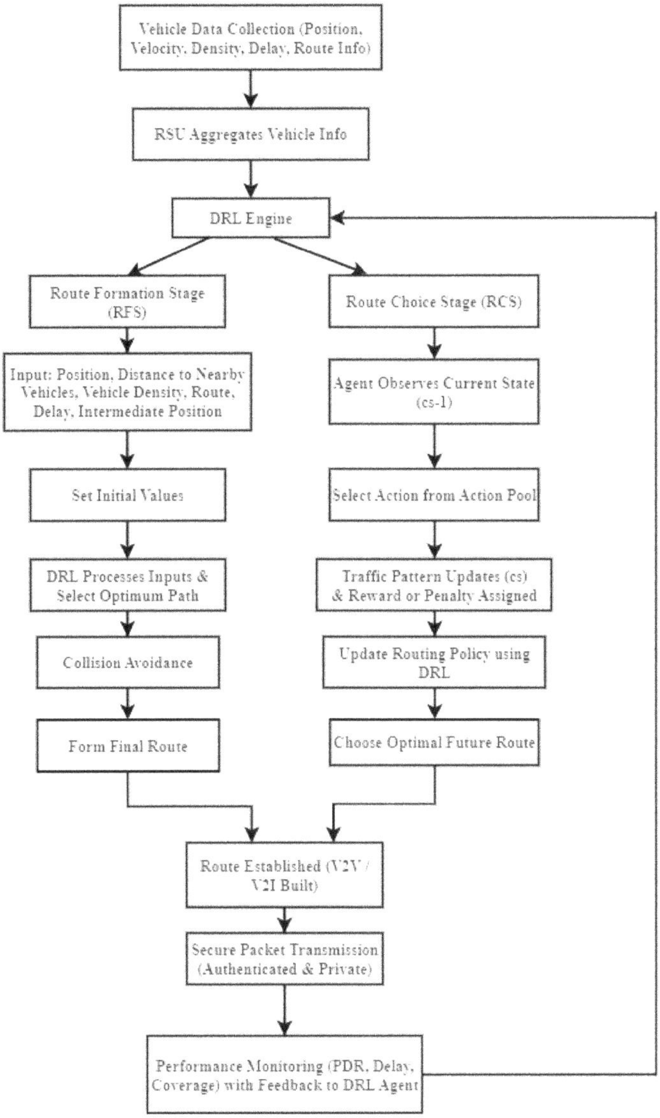


**Figure 4.1 Workflow of DRL Based Routing**

The proposed Algorithm (4.2) for the Route Choice Stage (RCS) is detailed as follows:

I. **Step 1:** At a given time 't', the agent employs the Traffic Pattern Map (TPM) and the optimal routes derived from observations of previous iterations. The purpose is to anticipate the future routing strategy, denoted as R(s). This R(s) inherently represents the expected outcome, whether it is a reward for an efficient path or a penalty for a suboptimal one.

II. **Step 2:** The observed TPM is then utilized to dynamically modify the current state, which is specifically denoted by TPM(s). Subsequently, the reward is calculated using equation (4.1) and (4.2) given in previous section i.e., RFS. A smaller ratio (approaching zero, or a larger negative value in this context) indicates a more efficient and less congested utilization of network resources relative to their optimal capacity, thereby yielding a higher reward. This implies that the DRL aims to identify and select routes that are not only optimal in terms of path length or directness but also highly efficient in their utilization of network bandwidth, which is essential for mitigating congestion and enhancing overall network performance.

III. **Step 3:** The DRL then employs its learned state and action function to forecast future routing methods. The ultimate goal is to maximize the expected cumulative reward, which directly leads to the identification and selection of the most advantageous and efficient routes within the dynamic VANET environment.

### 4.6.5 Experimental Setup and Performance Evaluation

In this section, the simulation environment, parameters, and measures of performance would be explained in which the suggested DRL routing mechanism is tested. It then shows and explains the obtained results of the experiments and compares the DRL approach to prior methods in the sphere of Packet Delivery Ratio (PDR) and End-to-End Delay (E2ED).

#### 4.6.5.1 Description of the Simulation Environment

The effectiveness of the given methodology was strictly calculated with the help of the well-known network simulator, NS-2. VanetMobiSim is a special mobility model generator of VANET, and VanetMobiSim was used to model operation of vehicle and truck within a metropolitan environment. The region of simulation was set to be a square area of 1000 meters on every side. The Roadside Units (RSUs) were to move with different speeds as their rate varied between 5 and 30 meters per second. Communication range of entities has been set at the maximum of 250 meters, taking into consideration the transmission power of the communication, so that effective communication coverage can be achieved within the said range of distance. The data packets were fixed at 512 bytes and the transmission source node used Constant Bit Rate (CBR) gnomic. The rates of data transmission at the receiving end depended on several things such as the nature of fading channel and distance between the vehicle sending and receiving data. Although the data connections and physical layers had an ability to use parametric settings on the simulation, the paper reported that the parameter value produced less effect on the machine learning phase and produced less attainable routes in the V2V communications with RSUs.

#### 4.6.5.2 Definition and Significance of Performance Metrics

Two primary performance metrics were utilized for evaluation:

A. **Packet Delivery Ratio (PDR):** Packet delivery ratio is used to measure the rate of success of the packet delivery, which is ratio of properly received packets to the number of packets post. A large PDR means that the routing protocol is more reliable, and able to ensure that data arrives where it is intended to.

B. **End-to-End Delay (E2ED):** This is the metric that is used to determine the average time taken by data packets to move through the network to the said final destination. When the E2ED is lower, the responsiveness (and the overall efficiency) of the network is higher and that is essential in the context of time-sensitive applications in VANETs.

### 4.6.6 Comparison with Existing Techniques and Discussion of Results

The outlined DRL algorithm was strictly tested in defending two widely used machine learning algorithms: Collaborative Learning Automata Routing (CLAR) and Support Vector Machine (SVM). The fact that DRL was able to outperform in all levels of RSU coverage and vehicle density speaks directly to the robustness and flexibility of the protocol that directly counters the inherent problem of VANETs that is its sensitive nature. This consistent high performance in the demanding and changing network environments proves that the DRL is adaptive in nature, which makes it one of the most suitable approaches to resolve the intricate dynamics of VANETs.

#### 4.6.6.1 Packet Delivery Ratio (PDR)

The DRL mechanism demonstrated a significant enhancement in the transmission coverage area, leading to improved PDR. Network performance, specifically PDR, consistently improved across all measured metrics as the RSU coverage area expanded. The proposed DRL approach achieved a higher PDR compared to both the SVM and CLAR methods, as detailed in Table 4.1and figure

4.1. Quantitatively, the DRL technique yielded an average 5% improvement in PDR over the existing CLAR method, primarily attributed to its effective tracking of connectivity between units via announcement messages. A key observation was that sending control signals between RSUs and vehicle units proved more reliable than direct vehicle-to-vehicle (V2V) communication.

**Table 4.1. Comparison between Coverage Ratio and Packet Delivery Ratio**

| RSU Coverage Ratio (%) | SVM (%) | CLAR (%) | DRL (%) |
|---|---|---|---|
| 30 | 81.27 | 83.71 | 86.8 |
| 40 | 84.63 | 85.9 | 89.53 |
| 50 | 88.54 | 91.22 | 93.91 |
| 60 | 92.45 | 94.75 | 96.01 |
| 70 | 94.05 | 97.81 | 98.11 |

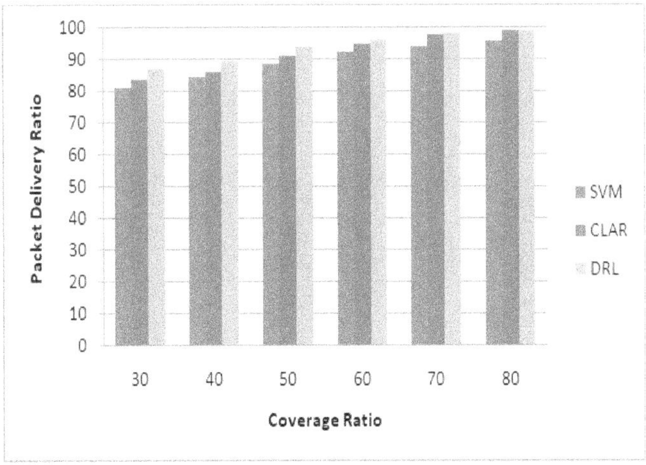

**Figure 4.2 Comparison between Coverage Ratio and Packet Delivery Ratio**

When analyzing PDR results based on vehicle density, the proposed DRL method also showed strong performance. As shown in Table 4.2 and figure 4.3, when compared to the current CLAR approach, the proposed method is described as "6.5% more expensive". In the context of Packet Delivery Ratio, "expensive" here refers to a superior performance, indicating a higher PDR, rather than increased cost or overhead. This interpretation aligns with the overall positive findings regarding DRL's efficacy. The dispersed nature of alternative architectures was noted as a factor contributing to their unreliability. Significantly, the utilization of command messages by RSUs resulted in a substantial 23% increase in PDR when compared to conventional approaches.

**Table 4.2 Comparison between Packet Delivery Ratio and Vehicle Density**

| Vehicle Density | SVM (%) | PDR CLAR (%) | DRL (%) |
|---|---|---|---|
| High | 88.9 | 90.48 | 92.54 |
| Low | 81.01 | 88.58 | 90.22 |

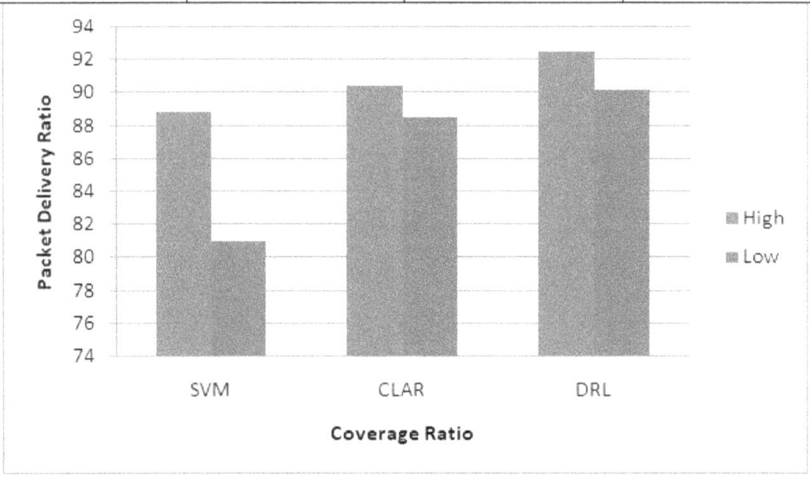

**Figure 4.3 Comparison between Packet Delivery Ratio and Vehicle Density**

#### 4.6.6.2End-to-End Delay (E2ED)

The results clearly demonstrated that RSU coverage has a significant impact on the delays experienced when forwarding packets from one RSU to another. A crucial finding was that decreasing the total area for transmission significantly lessened the associated delays. Table 4.3 and figure 4.3, illustrates the End-to-End Delay performance across varying RSU coverage ratios. Table 4.4 and figure 4.4 presents the End-to-End Delay results based on vehicle density.

**Table 4.3. Comparison between Coverage Ratio and End-To-End Delay**

| RSU Coverage Ratio (%) | SVM (ms) | CLAR (ms) | DRL (ms) |
|---|---|---|---|
| 30 | 14.61 | 5.43 | 5.11 |
| 40 | 14.31 | 5.21 | 4.46 |
| 50 | 13.98 | 5.92 | 4.17 |
| 60 | 13.82 | 4.67 | 3.98 |
| 70 | 13.66 | 3.98 | 2.61 |
| 80 | 12.63 | 3.84 | 2.15 |

**Table 4.4. Comparison between End-To-End Delay and Vehicle Density**

| Vehicle Density | SVM (ms) | CLAR (ms) | DRL (ms) |
|---|---|---|---|
| High | 11.58 | 3.48 | 2.64 |
| Low | 22.47 | 6.1 | 5.74 |

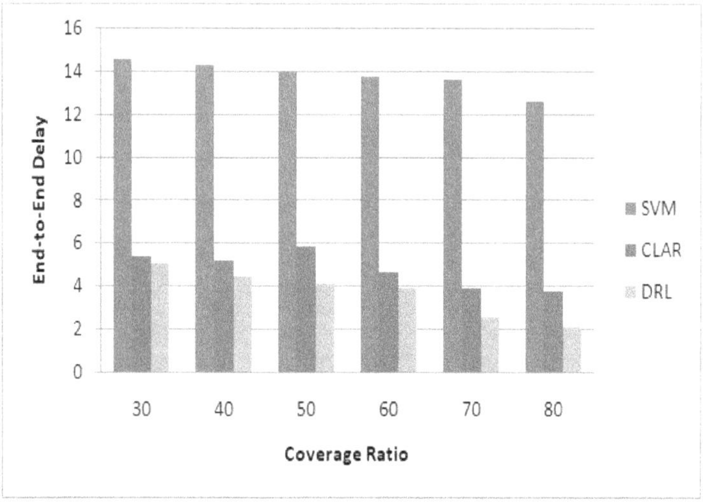


**Figure 4.4 Comparison between Coverage Ratio and End-to-End Delay**

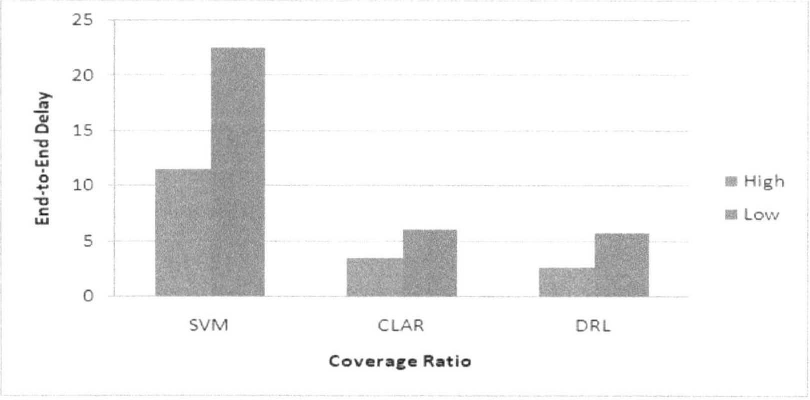


**Figure 4.5 Comparison between End-to-End Delay and Vehicle Density**

## 4.7 Quantitative and Qualitative Interpretation of Performance Improvement

The experimental results consistently demonstrate that the proposed DRL method significantly outperforms both SVM and CLAR across all evaluated metrics: Packet Delivery Ratio (PDR) and End-to-End Delay (E2ED). This superior performance holds true under varying conditions, including different RSU coverage ratios and fluctuating vehicle densities. The quantitative gains in PDR, such as an average 5% improvement over CLAR and a 23% increase over conventional approaches through RSU command messages, underscore DRL's enhanced reliability in delivering packets. The substantial reduction in End-to-End Delay, exemplified by a decrease from 14.61ms for SVM at 30% RSU coverage to 5.11ms for DRL, and from 22.47ms for SVM at low vehicle density to 5.74ms for DRL, highlights DRL's effectiveness in minimizing communication latency, which is critical for real-time VANET applications.

The achieved reliability of the communication between the RSU and the vehicle, in comparison to V2V connectivity, is recognized as one of the reasons why the DRL is effective. This observation indicates that although Vehicular Ad hoc Networks would generally be envisaged as nothing but ad-hoc (V2V) network, the DRLs functionality could greatly be augmented by utilizing the inherent stability and broader coverage as well as higher processing power typically offered by Roadside Units (RSUs). This means that there may be a dependency: when there are few RSUs deployed or when there are only vehicles that communicate with each other, then the performance of the DRL may not be as stable as in this case. This finding presents an important future research direction: understanding how DRL can be modified or otherwise made stronger to be able to continue to demonstrate a robust and efficient performance in diverse or even extreme RSU sparse or V2V set-ups, or under what hybrid communication schemes performance can take advantage of infrastructure availability to best purpose.

## 4.8 Summery

This chapter covered the highly important issues of routing efficiency and security in Vehicular Ad hoc Networks (VANETs) in the general context of and in the light of Internet of Things (IoT). It has been established that current routing and security protocols do not always perform well since VANETs are highly dynamic, only find local optimization in routing, and a key separation between security protocols and important Quality of Service (QoS) measures. It is in this respect that the Deep Reinforcement Learning (DRL)-based routing protocol proposed provides a solution to these complex challenges, as it is a robust solution. The DRL mechanism thus has the satisfactory property of both immediate, localized forwarding of packets, and strategic, long-term route optimization, by performing two stages of the same process, which are the Route Formation Stage (RFS) and the Route Choice Stage (RCS). The advanced reward mechanism aimed at the balanced combination of throughput and efficient use of resources contributes to the avoidance of network congestion and a stable and high-performance of communication. Moreover, DRL capability to work despite the known inconsistencies of the GPS data shows its flexibility of thinking in a complex spatial-temporal association. Within experimental analyses that utilize both NS-2 and VanetMobiSim, results lead to the same conclusion that the proposed DRL approach fares significantly better than other traditional methods such as SVM and CLAR based on most performance parameters. The DRL performed well in terms of Packet Delivery Ratio (PDR) and significant minimization of End-To-End Delay (E2ED) with different RSU ratio of coverage and vehicle density. Such quantitative advantages highlight that DRL is more reliable and responsive, which is confirmation of its ability to manage the unpredictable nature of VANETs. The reliability observed by the RSU-to-vehicle communication in facilitating the success of DRL also indicates the usefulness of integrated infrastructure in streamlining the performance of ad-hoc networks.

Future directions of the proposed research are to incorporate other features like anonymity, mutual authentication, and intractability to lower both communication and computation costs, where this type of research can be crucial in finite applications such as e-healthcare, i-transportation, and smart ecosystems. Also, security could be enhanced with a trust-based intrusion detection system, as part of a cooperative VANET scheme. Use of advanced deep learning algorithms into the routing mechanism has a potential of further increasing speed of computation in V2I communication in real time applications.

The above work is published as research paper "Maurya, P., Devi, S., Yadav, R. K., Saran, M., and Tripathi, U. N. (2023). An Efficient Routing Mechanism for IoT using Deep Learning." i-manager's Journal on IoT and Smart Automation, 1(2), 7-15.

# CHAPTER 5

# AN INTEGRATED APPROACH TO OPTIMIZE THE INTRUSION DETECTION SYSTEM IN SDN BASED ON FEATURE SELECTION AND DEEP LEARNING TECHNIQUES

# CHAPTER 5

# AN INTEGRATED APPROACH TO OPTIMIZE THE INTRUSION DETECTION SYSTEM IN SDN BASED ON FEATURE SELECTION AND DEEP LEARNING TECHNIQUES

In the chapter, an optimized approach to streamline Intrusion Detection Systems (IDS) on Software-Defined Networking (SDN) is depicted through feature selection and deep learning processes. It introduces the architectural issues of SDN, the shortcomings of conventional security, and the approach to the solution of architecture, result of the experiments and the insights about the future secure networks.

## 5. Introduction

Software-Defined Networking (SDN) is a revolutionizing technology in the design of a network as it introduces a paradigm shift in the operationalization and control of networks. The paradigm has attained modular, flexible, and efficient network management through decoupling of the control plane and data plane. SDN centralizes the control of the network and hidden the underlying infrastructure itself, thus making it possible to enjoy dynamic configuration capabilities resulting in great scalability, flexibility, and administrative ease. In its essence, SDN is a combination of several main components.

***Control Plane***, which is commonly represented by SDN Controller operates as a centralized network brain that determines flow control to the different networking devices such as switches and routers using protocols like OpenFlow. Such centralization simplifies implementation of policies and network set up. On the other hand, there is the ***Data Plane*** which includes forwarding equipment (physical or virtual switches and routers) and is concerned with relaying packets in real-time according to instructions given by the controller. Northbound APIs forms a communication connection between the *SDN controller* and the upper tier applications via which the network can be programmed, and which provide an interface to orchestration and automation tools. Finally, Southbound APIs, like OpenFlow, are protocols that the controller uses to communicate with data plane devices to have fine control over the forwarding plane.

In addition to the strong benefits posed by SDN, architectural changes make new and grave security risks. Centralized control and the open API of the SDN is designed to raise the level of the risk of the breaking into the network. Since the SDN controller acts as a central element, there lies the possibility of making it an expensive target by hackers, and that the nature of SDN being dynamic and programmable can be easily abused to cause some mischief. The requirement of more intelligent and adaptive methods is also highlighted by the fact that traditional security measures in a static, distributed network environment are a problem in this dynamic and programmable environment. In modern days, network security has been recognized as a paramount issue and much has not been done to rectify its many concerns even after decades of concentrated studies [75]. The current detection methods encounter a very high number of challenges such as failure to accurately detect a wide range of intrusion types, the inability to detect threats in encrypted traffic and shortcomings in detecting systemic attacks. Moreover, high-speed networks could easily intrude with the introduction of several intrusion detection processes, which serve to complicate intrusion detection to the extreme.

There exists a basic problem of SDN due to what can be perceived as a paradox of centralization. Although centralization of management of networks is celebrated as an efficiency, scale, and adjustability advantage, the same feature is a pathogen that creates a significant risk. Although the centralized controller can simplify the process of controlling, it concentrates risk and is thus concentrated in a single point and a desirable target to attack. Such architectural trade-off requires security measures to be capable of monitoring and securing such a centralized hub of control, stepping out of the old, distributed security paradigms.

In addition, SDN is dynamic and programmable and thus network settings and traffic patterns can be varied very quickly. Such fluidity makes non-dynamic, signature-based Traditional Intrusion Detection Systems (IDS) largely ineffective since new vectors of attack may appear then in a short time. The SDN security solutions will thus be required to have an inherent adaptability and learning abilities to match up with the dynamic threat environment as well as the network dynamism. The solution to this requirement is right at the hand of deep learning with its ability to automate the learning process, detecting sophisticated patterns of attack in real-time [76].

The present research is an effort to overcome these significant security concerns by developing a smart Intrusion Detection System (IDS) to use deep learning techniques to boost network safety in the SDN framework. The key research aims of the proposed work are: to solve the security concern generated by centralization of SDN; to capture the multi-dimensional behavior of the attack using deep learning models, namely CNN-LSTM; to lower the dimensionality of data and achieve high accuracy model using the technique of feature selection and removing of outliers; and to compare two optimized models, that yield accuracy up to 99.5% on In SDN dataset. The final goal will be to create a flexible and effective IDS system that will be able to secure real-time SDN infrastructure [77][78].

## 5.1 Overview of Intrusion Detection Systems and Deep Learning

Intrusion Detection Systems (IDS) are central in the protection of networks, where an IDS monitors the activities occurring within a network or an institution and examines it to detect signs of attacks that may lead to a breach of dependability, accessibility, confidentiality, or bypass of security measures. Attacks on any intrusion may come in either form of an external attacker, legitimate user with overuse of privileges, or individuals gaining new privileges without legal access. IDS are often referred to as the disciplines of technological security as their basic security system consists of the so-called intrusion alarms placed strategically in different areas across a network to identify the packets and their possible hazards. They do it by collating information through different systems and sources of information on their networks and then analyze the information that might be threats. The roles of an IDS go beyond providing information about risks and application of remedies to a threat that is already realized as well as recording of all significant events taking place in a network. Different types of IDS may have quite different protective boundaries, and they can protect one computer, just like a large network. As an example, a Network Intrusion Detection System (NIDS) is specialized to examine incoming traffic on the network whereas a Host Intrusion Detection (HIDS) scans the important files of the operating system. Some of the key classification methods of IDS are by their detection mechanism which may involve signature-based search; anomaly-based detection and reputation-based detection [79].

The traditional IDS are known to be less efficient in handling the new or dynamically changing threats since they usually rely on pre-existence signatures or protocols. This shortcoming highlights one of the most vital demands of modern networks i.e. moving on to anomaly-based detection, rather than signature-based detection. The mutation of malware and zero-day attacks are too fast in nature to work with the static databases that are used to maintain the signature databases. This issue is compounded by the highly dynamic network types such as SDN whose traffic patterns are highly volatile to such an extent that signature-based methods are not effective. Deep Learning (DL) as an effective subsection of Machine Learning (ML) can provide the solution with the further possibilities of pattern identification and anomaly detection. The ability of DL-based IDS to learn and detect threats previously unseen is a radical lifeline in advancing to proactive threat-based anomalous IDS learning, which is needed to achieve strong protection in dynamic and dynamic networks. With the addition of SDN, the deep learning-used intrusion detection systems have the potential of greatly enhancing the process of detecting threats and responding to them, performing this process by analyzing large amounts of data on the network to detect complex patterns of attacks [80].

The options of deep learning signify an important innovation to Artificial Neural Networks (ANN) in that the technique utilizes the complex calculation to make the algorithms recognize information representations via a number of levels of generalization. The techniques have a wide variety of uses which include network intrusion detection, network identification, and recognition of visual objects. Deep learning systems are able to be trained either in the unsupervised or supervised manner. There are a number of deep learning methods, which can be considered especially applicable to IDS [81] [82]:

A. **Convolutional Neural Networks (CNN):** Often trained in a supervised manner, CNNs are widely used for intrusion detection, demonstrating enhanced accuracy and system efficiency. They are considered the standard for computer vision applications, adept at organizing two-dimensional pictures and applied in areas like face recognition.
B. **Autoencoders:** These deep learning approaches are typically trained in an unsupervised manner. Auto-encoders are primarily utilized to analyze data encoding or representation,

particularly for dimensionality reduction, and are integrated with various other techniques for network intrusion detection.

C. **Deep Belief Networks (DBN):** A DBN is a deep learning algorithm that reconstructs its input using a collection of examples in an unsupervised manner, with its layers functioning as feature detectors. Following this initial learning phase, DBNs can be fine-tuned in a supervised manner for classification purposes. DBNs, including autoencoders and restricted Boltzmann machines (RBMs), are versatile, applicable to regression, feature learning, collaborative filtering, topic modeling, and dimensionality reduction.

D. **Recurrent Neural Networks (RNN):** RNNs are deep learning methodologies trained using both supervised and unsupervised techniques. They possess the unique ability to regulate internal memory to process arbitrary inputs, making them suitable for effective intrusion detection.

E. **CNN-LSTM:** This hybrid model combines the strengths of CNNs and Long Short-Term Memory (LSTM) networks (a type of RNN). CNNs excel at extracting relevant features from the "spatial" representation of network data, such as a snapshot of flow features. LSTMs are adept at understanding the "temporal" dependencies and sequences of these features over time, which is critical for detecting evolving attack patterns. This synergistic potential of hybrid deep learning architectures is a deliberate design choice to address the multi-dimensional nature of network intrusion detection, suggesting that complex cybersecurity problems often require integrated, multi-modal solutions that can capture different facets of the data, leading to more comprehensive and accurate threat detection [83].

F. **ResNet50:** This model is also employed in the study for comparative analysis.

## 5.2 Proposed Methodology for Optimized IDS in SDN Environments

The creation of an efficient Intrusion Detection System (IDS) of Software-Defined Networking (SDN) systems using deep learning would require a systematic approach that will involve gathering of data, model building, and thorough tests. The process takes root in the meticulous selection of an appropriate dataset that is indicative of the specific characteristics and difficulties that are characteristic of SDN systems. Thereafter, the model of deep learning is created to process the obtained data, and the main aim is to detect and classify different network breaches. The effectiveness of this model is then carefully evaluated under the traditional standards to prove its effectiveness in real life application. The rest of this systematic approach is described in the subsections below.

### 5.2.1 Dataset Description and Pre-processing

The paper employs the InSDN dataset [18] which is a collection of intrusion detection data that is specifically used in SDN. This data is large (and consists of more than 43,939 records) which includes benign (harmless) and malicious (unwanted) network traffic. The corrupted traffic consists of an extensive list of attack types, web attacks, password-guessing attacks, Botnet Traffic, probing, Denial of Service (DoS) attacks, and the Distributed Denial of Service (DoS) attacks. The original in the SDN data set is elaborate detailing 84 characteristics that give packet based and flow-based information. It is dogmatically comprehensive and fits the modeling trends of SDN-specific flows and attacks, which makes it the choice of tool when training and evaluating deep learning-based IDS algorithms in SDNs. Data cleaning and the data preparation included exploration data analysis (EDA) that was to provide a comprehensible image of the structure and the overall example of the dataset and the significant properties. To increase accuracy and efficiency of later models, several preprocessing procedures were completed. These were partitioning the categorical variables, the normalization of numerical variables using a specified range, and a method of removing redundant variables and features characterizing the constant value that would not add any significant variable to the learning process.

### 5.2.2 Outlier Detection and Removal using Local Outlier Factor (LOF)

A key step in the data preparation was to feature extraction of risks and outlier elimination, which were facilitated, with the Local Outlier Factor (LOF) method. LOF plays a crucial role in the detection of dataset outliers where variances in the local density of a particular data point are compared to those data which are nearest neighbors. Data point that has a much lower than average density compared to its neighbors can be said to be an outlier. A sequence of steps is involved when it comes to LOF:

I. **Identification of Neighbors:** LOF finds the nearest neighbors of each data point which are commonly known as k-nearest neighbors (k-NN) and a range of distance functions are used.

II. **Reachability Distance:** The reachability distance is calculated to measure the distances between two points while accounting for the density of neighboring sites. This helps determine if a point is truly isolated from its surrounding points. The equation for Reachability Distance is given in equation (5.1).

$$\boldsymbol{Reach\_Distance_{(p,o)} = \max(k - distance(o), distance(p,o)} \qquad \textbf{(5.1)}$$

Where, Distance (p, o) denotes the actual distance between point p and o, and k-distance (o) represents the k-distance of positions.

III. **Local Reachability Density (LRD):** LRD is computed by LOF to estimate the density around a specific site. If a point is surrounded by fewer points than its neighbors, its Local Reachability Density will be reduced. The equation for Local Reachability Density is given in equation (5.2).

$$\boldsymbol{LRD(p)} = \frac{1}{\frac{1}{k}\sum_{o \in n_{k(p)}}(\boldsymbol{Reach\_Distance}_{(p,o)})} \qquad \textbf{(5.2)}$$

IV. **Calculation of LOF Score:** Points are ultimately rated by comparing their Local Reachability Density (LRD) to the LRDs of their neighbors, as defined by the LOF score. A high LOF score indicates an unusual occurrence, signifying that its local density is considerably lower than that of its neighbors. The equation for the LOF Score is:

$$\boldsymbol{LOF}_{(p)} = \frac{\sum_{o \in n_{k(p)}} \frac{\boldsymbol{LRD}_{(o)}}{\boldsymbol{LRD}_{(p)}}}{\frac{1}{k}\sum_{o \in n_{k(p)}}(\boldsymbol{Reach}_{\boldsymbol{Distance}_{(p,o)}})} \qquad \textbf{(5.3)}$$

In this equation, LRD(o) refers to the local reachability density of neighbor o, and LRD(p) represents the reachability density of point p.

Elbow method was used to find the best number of neighbors (k) that the algorithm using LOF should have and the most appropriate value of k was found to be 20. The target of the strategy is where the mean LOF values will stop changing with a variety of k values, which will allow striking the right balance between accurately detecting true outliers and minimizing false positives. Once the LOF predictions are accumulated, the outlier values which are normally equal to -1 (denoting risk) and 1 (denoting inliers) are tackled in a binary format which gives a clear indicator on whether an individual data point is a risky data point or otherwise.

This method of optimally searching the data to come up with the best model is a keystone of this method. The data are increasingly filtered as the steps are followed one after the other in the EDA and preprocessing, outlier removal, feature selection. Still, every stage is an extension of the prior one, which means that the data used to train the deep learning models will be clean, normalized, and pertinent. Careful data engineering is essential because low-quality data or unrelated features were bound to compromise the overall model performance so that no matter the architectural deep learning design, poor results lay ahead. This further supports the idea that the effectiveness of more sophisticated models is largely dependent on whether the data used in the process has been engineered in a highly unified fashion, once again reaffirming the notion of the Data being involved in a symbiotic relationship with the model.

### 5.2.3 Feature Engineering and Selection using Recursive Feature Elimination (RFE)

The process of feature selection and reduction will be paramount in improving the effectiveness of Intrusion Detection Systems (IDS), especially where complex SDN scenarios have to employ a data set such as in SDN. The problem with high-dimensional data is that it can be affected by the so-called curse of dimensionality that makes computing more complex, prolongs the training of the model, and may lead to overfitting. In order to reduce such problems,

It used Recursive Feature Elimination (RFE) as one of the strategic methods. RFE effectively removes the least significant features in a highly structured manner, according to their effect on the effectiveness of the model and leaving the most discriminating attributes to the model.

By using this advanced technique in terms of reducing dimensionality on the In SDN dataset, dimensionality was reduced significantly. The two optimized and distinct sets of features identified through the process were with 48 features, and 30 key features respectively. These pruned sets were constructed with the aim of enhancing the performance of deep learning models since it would have a shorter and more pertinent input space. Such a dimensionality reduction of strategies is critical to the balance between accuracy and computational costs. The study hopes to enhance the accuracy, minimize the training duration and minimize the memory requirements which are essential when putting an IDS deployment in a resource-limited or high-throughput SDN infrastructures by relying on a few features.

### 5.2.4 Deep Learning Classification

Following the comprehensive data preparation phase—which included pre-processing, outlier removal, feature selection, and the splitting of data into training and test sets—the study proceeded to the model training stage. The primary objective at this juncture was to assess the effectiveness of various deep learning algorithms and identify the most efficient option for intrusion detection in SDN. The deep learning models selected and employed in this research for classification were:

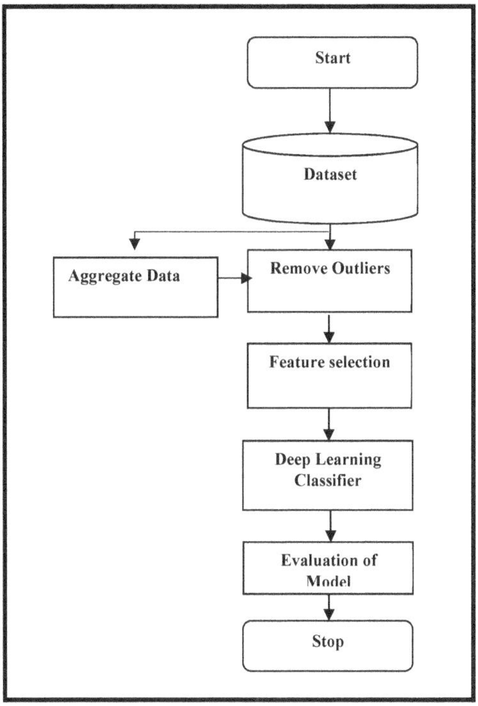


**Figure 5.1 Workflow of Intrusion Detection System using Deep Learning**

A. **Deep Belief Network (DBN):** As a deep learning algorithm, DBN reconstructs its input using a collection of examples in an unsupervised manner, with its layers acting as feature detectors. Post-learning, DBNs can be trained in a supervised mode for classification. They are versatile, finding applications in regression, feature learning, collaborative filtering, topic modeling, and dimensionality reduction.

B. **ResNet50:** This is a widely recognized convolutional neural network architecture, included in the study for comparative performance analysis.

C. **CNN-LSTM:** It is a hybrid architecture which is a combination of the advantages of CNN-based network and LSTM-based network. CNNs perform well with spatial data and are typically applied to computer vision in organizing two dimensional pictures. LSTMs are a kind of Recurrent Neural Network (RNN) that can control internal memory to produce arbitrary sequential outputs, which lends it to analytics characterized by temporal dependency in the data.

In such a way it was possible to critically analyze the performance of various architecture options in deep learning when applied to the problem of SDN intrusion detection, in particular, in combination with advanced data preparation methods.

### 5.2.5 Experimental Setup and Performance Evaluation

The experimental phase involved a rigorous setup to train and test the selected deep learning models on the prepared InSDN dataset. After the comprehensive data preparation, which included pre-processing, outlier removal, and feature selection, the dataset was split into training and testing sets. The models were then trained on the training data and evaluated on the unseen test data. The core objective of this evaluation was to assess the performance of the proposed Intrusion Detection System (IDS) using various deep learning techniques. To understand the impact of feature selection on detection accuracy, speed, and resource effectiveness, the evaluation was conducted using two distinct feature sets: one comprising 48 features and another with 30 features, both derived from the original InSDN dataset.

#### 5.2.5.1 Performance Metrics Defined

The effectiveness of the deep learning models was exhaustively determined with a set of generic comparative metrics of classification, which help to fully comprehend the efficiency of the models:

a. **Accuracy:** This provides the percentage correct instances (the true positive and the true negative) regarding the actual number of instances. It gives a general indicator of rightness.

$$\textbf{Accuracy} = \frac{\text{True Positive + True Negative}}{\text{True Positive + True Negative+ False Positive + False Negative}} \quad \textbf{(5.1)}$$

b. **Precision:** It is the percentage of correct positive predictions to all those predicted positives. Precision refers to how the model can avoid the problem of false alarms which is vital in the cases of security pursuits.

$$\textbf{Precision} = \frac{\text{True Positive}}{\text{True Positive + False Positive}} \quad \textbf{(5.2)}$$

c. **Recall (Sensitivity):** This foreshadows the percentage of the positive predictions made among all real positive signals (True Positives / (False Negatives + True Positives)). Recall represents the capacity of the model to recognize every real intrusion, by reducing the unseen threats.

$$\textbf{Recall} = \frac{\text{True Positive}}{\text{True Positive + False Negative}} \quad \textbf{(5.3)}$$

d. **F1-Score:** The F1-Score is the harmonic mean of Precision and Recall, calculated using equation (5.4). It provides a balanced measure, particularly useful for datasets where class distribution might be imbalanced, offering a single score that considers both false positives and false negatives.

$$\textbf{F1-Score} = \frac{2*(\text{Precision} * \text{Recall})}{(\text{Precision} + \text{Recall})} \qquad \textbf{(5.4)}$$

### 5.2.5.2 Comparative Analysis of Models with 48 Features

The comparison of the three deep learning models, ResNet50, Deep Belief Network (DBN) and CNN-LSTM was initially performed on the feature set that contained 48 specifically selected features. The findings, as it has been articulated in Table 5.1, emphasize the effectiveness of every architecture.

As evident from Table 5.1, the **CNN-LSTM** model achieved the highest performance across all metrics. It recorded an exceptional accuracy of 99.5%, a precision of 99.6%, a recall of 98.3%, and an F1-score of 99.0%. These figures demonstrate the model's superior ability to minimize both false positives and false negatives effectively when classifying network data as either benign or malicious.

The **Deep Belief Network (DBN)** also exhibited strong performance, with an accuracy of 97.1%, precision of 98.6%, a notably high recall of 99.3%, and an F1-score of 98.5%. The high recall for DBN indicates its success in detecting actual intrusions, though it presented a slightly higher number of false positives compared to CNN-LSTM.

**Table 5.1: Comparing Various Deep Learning Classifiers for CNN-LSTM, Deep Belief Network (DBN), and ResNet50 with 48 features**

| Model | Parameter | Values (%) |
|---|---|---|
| With 48 Features | | |
| **ResNet50** | Accuracy | 97.0 |
| | Precision | 97.0 |
| | Recall | 99.0 |
| | F1-Score | 98.0 |
| **Deep Belief Network (DBN)** | Accuracy | 97.1 |
| | Precision | 98.6 |
| | Recall | 99.3 |
| | F1-Score | 98.5 |
| **CNN-LSTM** | Accuracy | 99.5 |
| | Precision | 99.6 |
| | Recall | 98.3 |
| | F1-Score | 99.0 |

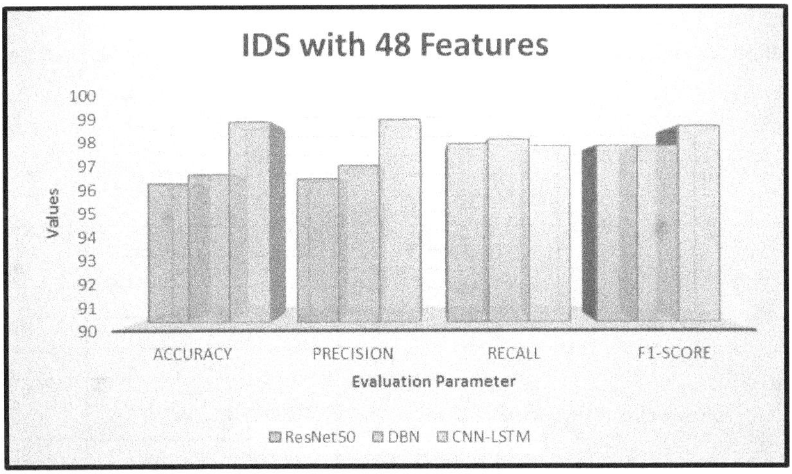


**Figure 5.2 Comparing Outcome for Proposed Models using InSDN dataset with 48 Features**

**ResNet50**, while demonstrating efficiency, yielded the lowest metrics among the three models. It achieved an accuracy of 97.0%, precision of 97.0%, recall of 99.0%, and an F1-score of 98.0%. These findings collectively suggest that the inclusion of a richer set of features (48 features) generally improves detection rates and provides more contextual information, which is particularly beneficial for powerful architectures like CNN-LSTM.

### 5.2.5.3 Comparative Analysis of Models with 30 Features

To assess the trade-off between detection performance and model complexity, the same deep learning models were analyzed using a smaller set of 30 features, which were carefully selected through recursive feature elimination. The results for this configuration are presented in Table 5.2.

**Table 5.2: Comparing Various Deep Learning Classifiers for CNN-LSTM, Deep Belief Network (DBN), and ResNet50 with 30 features**

| Model | Parameter | Values (%) |
|---|---|---|
| **With 30 Features** | | |
| **ResNet50** | Accuracy | 96.3 |
| | Precision | 96.5 |
| | Recall | 98.1 |
| | F1-Score | 98.0 |
| **Deep Belief Network (DBN)** | Accuracy | 96.7 |
| | Precision | 97.1 |
| | Recall | 98.3 |
| | F1-Score | 98.0 |
| **CNN-LSTM** | Accuracy | 99.1 |
| | Precision | 99.2 |
| | Recall | 98.0 |
| | F1-Score | 98.9 |

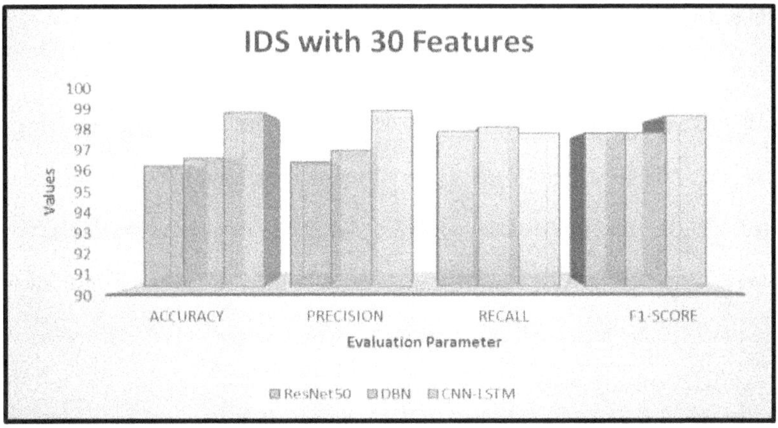


**Figure 5.3 Comparing Outcome for Proposed Models using InSDN dataset with 30 Features**

Here, once again, CNN-LSTM achieved best results, however, this time with a slight decline in comparison to their results with a 48-feature model. It attained an accuracy of 99.1 percent, precision of 99.2 percent, recall of 98.0 percent and F1-score of 98.9 percent. This proves the high flexibility of the model and its good performance using a smaller number of input features.

Both DBN and ResNet50 were affected by a minor drop in performance as well when using the 30-feature set. DBN recorded accuracy, precision, recall and F1-score of 96.7, 97.1, 98.3 and 98.0 respectively. The ResNet50 achieved the accuracy of 96.3 percent, precision of 96.5 percent, recall of 98.1 percent and the F1-score of 98.0 percent.

This observance of the robustness of CNN-LSTM under different feature dimensionality is very crucial. It recorded the most accurate performance when it comes to both features 48 and 30. Its total performance fell a little lower as compared to its competitors, but it had more features and was still better off than the rest. This is indicative of the fact that CNN-LSTM architecture, with its tendency to capture spatial and temporal relationships is more resistant and flexible to changes in the dimensionality of incoming data A model that is simpler with fewer features and high performance would be desired in practice in a dynamic environment such as SDN, since the overhead required to execute the model would be lower along with other parameters such as speed of inference. The fact that CNN-LSTM was consistently superior serves as a validation of its promise as an architecturally desirable model to be applied in near- to real-time scenarios with limited resources in mind where accuracy matters most in IDS.

#### 5.2.5.4 Impact of Hyperparameter Optimization using Optuna

Further, to enhance the performance of the models, an autonomous hyperparameter optimization framework, Optuna, was used. Such an approach was very beneficial in exploring the hyperparameter space that is so large and features important parameters such as learning rate, number of layers, and dropout rates.

The advantages of the use of Optuna were huge. It made the models much more accurate and at the same time it lowered overfitting and minimized time spent on training. On a consistent basis, the models were trained to be more accurate than the default models after tuning the hyperparameters using Optuna. This shows the importance of post-architectural optimization that can be defined as hyperparameter tuning. The fact that deep learning models are complex suggests their performance is quite sensitive to the hyperparameters. Poor parameters may result in problems such as overfitting, underfitting or slow convergence such that it invalidates the gains of architecture. Auto-optimizer systems, such as Optuna, explore this huge parameter space in a systematic but still brute-force fashion to identify near-optimal parameters, and a specific phase of fine-tuning the internal learning process is required to achieve optimal results in production applications in deep learning. This reiterates that state-of-the-art findings usually occur through the end-to-end optimization process involving data preparation, model choice, and hyperparameter optimization.

### 5.2.6 Discussion of Experimental Findings and Implications

The results of conducting the experiment are of high importance in the further elaboration of the effective Intrusion Detection Systems (IDS) in Software-Defined Networking (SDN) areas. The findings all indicate the strong importance of feature engineering in high-dimensional data applications as in this case SDN, the recurrent formulation of the CNN-LSTM model consistently producing the best results with changes in feature set sizes; and the fact that hyperparameter tuning is the key in providing the best possible set of classifier settings.

The performance of CNN-LSTM model is much better and is a robust conclusion. In both datasets, the 48-feature and 30-feature, CNN-LSTM performed the best in all main indicators, which are accuracy, precision, recall, and F1-score. It had an accuracy of a high of 99.5% because 48 features were discussed and it was very important to note it had high accuracy of 99.1% even when the features were reduced to 30. It means that the model has the outstanding ability to reduce both false positive and false negative database instances in classifying the network traffic either malicious or benign. This good performance is credited to the ability of CNN-LSTM to perform deep sequential learning, allowing it to efficiently learn both the spatial and time characteristics of traffic that is extremely dynamic in nature in SDN environment.

The effect of feature selection on accuracy of detection and resources required to conduct the same is another important implication. In the research, the comparisons of those models trained on 48 features and 30 features (both using the initial 84 features of the In SDN datasets) were made explicitly. The findings show that features within a dataset are important and can typically increase the rate of detection depending on the amount of contextual information available during the classification process since the accuracy of the CNN-LSTM model is increased when using 48 features (99.5%) as compared to the 30 features (99.1%). On the other hand, although the accuracy was again very high with 30 features, the decrease in precision and recall rates in the case of DBN and ResNet50 indicated that perhaps there was some marginal information that was lost with lower numbers of characteristics. Nevertheless, the approach used also points out that features selection and reduction are also bases to enhance the efficiency of IDS systems. The Recursive Feature Elimination (RFE) method used in this point was demonstrated to be able to extract important features and use low time complexity (averaging approximately 0.62 μs) and less memory resource.

This leads to a significant understanding: the practical viability of high-performance IDS in resource-constrained SDN environments. The CNN-LSTM model's achievement of 98.9% accuracy with only 30 features, coupled with the low computational complexity and memory usage of the feature selection process, directly translates to lower computational demands, faster inference times, and a smaller memory footprint. This makes the solution highly practical and deployable in real-time, high-throughput SDN infrastructures where traditional, resource-heavy IDS might struggle. This moves the research beyond purely theoretical performance metrics to address practical deploy ability, indicating a viable path for implementing robust IDS in real-world, dynamic, and potentially resource-limited SDN settings.

A significant role was also discovered to be played by hyperparameter optimization with Optuna. As an independent hyperparameter optimization solution, Optuna was able to search better alongside the hyperparameter space, which involved hyperparameters like dropout rates, learning rate, number of layers, etc. This process of optimization resulted in higher model accuracy and, at the same time, minimized overfitting and training time. The hyperparameter-optimized models were performing better on a regular basis as compared to the default settings. This highlights that to make the highest possible performance in the targeted application of deep learning, the best choice of the algorithm should not be the final task, and a careful data engineering procedure is not enough; it is the turn to carefully train the inner learning process of the model.

Moreover, the findings show the dynamics between sophistication of architecture and data pruning to optimize the systems. The fact that CNN-LSTM model outperformed, despite having fewer features than the initial collections, can indicate that even though RFE is an effective way to truncate data, a strong network model can get away with some of the loss of input. This shows how the following is a symbiotic relationship: a powerful architecture may be able to perform well by using pruned data, and likewise, pruned data can help the powerful architecture to perform better. This leads to the optimal system design approach of investing into highly sophisticated deep learning architecture (such as CNN-LSTM) which has great feature learning capabilities in combination with intelligent feature engineering to provide a good trade-off where high detection accuracy is achieved with improvement of resource efficiency such that an effective balance is reached of the IDS solution in a more complex network environment.

### 5.7 Summery

The findings of the proposed study fulfilled the efforts of designing an efficient, flexible, and dynamic intrusion detection system through the combination of the reduced feature selection method and deep learning algorithm. The main success of this study was to present an easy to use feature selection criterion of dimensionality reduction, which was specially devised to retrieve the most significant features of the data set. The given method can be described as a combination of Recursive Feature Elimination (RFE) and a Local Outlier Factor (LOF) simplified Mutual Information feature selection, which allows finding the most relevant features to be used during classifier training. The present feature selection process proved to be highly efficient, with a low computer time complexity, which is around 0.62 μs, on average and with less memory usage.

The focus areas of this study are highlighted by the performance metrics that have been realized here. The CNNLSTM model also accomplished a high accuracy rate of 99.5 when trained on a reduced set of 48 features out of the actual 84 original features of the In SDN dataset in multiclass classification after going through the deep learning algorithm of comparison. Moreover, an accuracy of 98.9% has been achieved, or using an even smaller set of only 30 (out of 84) features of the In SDN dataset, which serves as additional evidence of the powerful potential of the CNN-LSTM model.

Nonetheless, improvement in granular architectural optimization of deep learning has been an aspect requiring significant research despite these high rates of performance. The authors recommend that future research focuses on the optimization of the architecture of the deep learning model such that the number of neurons in each layer will be optimized as well as the number of layers in every one of the concealed layers. It means that even such near-perfect outcomes can be mostly improved with architectural exploration, which is done carefully, indicating that the use of automated neural architecture search (NAS) approaches would likely move this process even quicker.

Beyond core detection it can be assumed that the changing nature of IDS research proposes an extended context. Although high effectiveness in the accuracy and efficiency of detection was the main concern in this research, high accuracy detection system alone does not comprise a comprehensive security solution. After the intrusion is identified, response mechanisms are the next obvious thing to take. Further work in the area of SDN-based IDS is also expected to go beyond the fundamental detection mechanism to a more complete security lifecycle, such as the integration of the IDS with other automated response systems, explanation AI (XAI) techniques so that decisions about detection can be better understood, and the use of a federated learning or edge computing paradigm to enable the distributed and privacy-preserving deployment of IDS in large-scale SDN. This developmental trend puts the research in terms of a component level solution to a full system level combination.

The above work is published as research paper entitled "An Integrated Approach to Optimize the Intrusion Detection System in SDN based on Feature Selection and Deep Learning Techniques" in International Journal of Computer Sciences and Engineering (IJCSE) Vol.13, Issue.5, pp.01-05, May 2025 ISSN: 2347-2693. Available online at: www.ijcseonline.org

# CHAPTER 6

# DYNAMIC OPTIMIZED QOS- AWARE ROUTING USING INTEGRATION OF PATICLE SWARM OPTIMIZATION WITH GRAPH NEURAL NETWORK

# CHAPTER 6

# DYNAMIC OPTIMIZED QoS- AWARE ROUTING USING INTEGRATION OF PATICLE SWARM OPTIMIZATION WITH GRAPH NEURAL NETWORK

## Introduction

An era of widespread connection has been brought in by the growth of the Internet2 of Things (IoT), which allows a wide range of devices in various industries, such as smart homes, healthcare, and transportation, to easily communicate and work together. Effective and dependable data transmission is essential to this networked environment, and it is a function that is heavily relies on strong routing protocols. Routing in IoT networks, however, poses difficult problems, especially in heterogeneous contexts where devices have wide differences in energy levels, processing capacity, and communication ranges. These challenges are made even more difficult by dynamic network conditions, such as irregular node failures and shifting traffic patterns, which call for extremely flexible and effective routing solutions. Since the Internet of Things is present in many important industries, routing inefficiencies could have a significant influence on real-world applications like patient monitoring in the medical field or the security of autonomous car navigation. These applications' importance makes routing more than just a networking problem; it's a social and economic issue, which emphasizes how urgently robust and intelligent routing solutions are needed [85].

**6.1 Problem Statement:** Traditional Routing's Issues in Dynamic, Heterogeneous IoT Dynamic Source Routing (DSR) and Ad-hoc On-demand Distance Vector (AODV), two traditional routing algorithms, usually fall short because they are unable to adjust to real-time network changes. As a result, these traditional methods are unable to ensure optimal performance, especially in the diverse and complex IoT contexts that are always changing. Increased latency, higher energy consumption, and an uneven load distribution throughout the network are all consequences of these underlying limits, which show up as notable inefficiencies across important Quality of Service (QoS) metrics [86]. Achieving low latency for time-sensitive applications, preserving high dependability for crucial data transmission, and reducing energy usage to extend the operational lifespan of battery-operated devices are all competing issues that must be carefully balanced for effective routing in Internet of Things networks. Traditional algorithms' inability to adapt to the fundamental dynamism and heterogeneity that characterize present IoT networks is a fundamental problem, not just a result of their subpar performance. This implies that a more fundamental paradigm shift in routing approach is necessary to effectively satisfy these changing needs, and that small adjustments to current systems are insufficient.

### 6.2 Motivation for Advanced, Adaptive Solutions

The stated drawbacks of existing methods highlight the urgent need for advanced techniques that can integrate global optimization with real-time flexibility. Therefore, the need to address these ongoing issues and satisfy the many and quickly expanding needs of modern IoT networks is what leads this research.

### 6.3 Proposed PSO-GNN Hybrid Approach and its Core Contribution

This thesis suggests a novel hybrid routing mechanism that combines PSO with a GNN architecture in order to overcome the issues that have been observed. This method uses a GNN to simulate the Internet of Things network as a dynamic graph, with nodes standing in for individual devices and edges for communication links. By learning from a variety of node and link characteristics, including as current latency, available bandwidth, and real-time energy levels, the GNN is intended to forecast the best routing routes. PSO then optimizes these GNN-predicted routes according to important QoS criteria including energy efficiency, latency, and reliability. This robust combination uses PSO's optimization capabilities to find the most efficient routes based on predetermined QoS criteria and GNNs' prediction capabilities to analyze and simulate challenging network dynamics. In order to ensure optimal performance, greatly increase routing efficiency, and provide scalability even in large and complex IoT contexts, the suggested hybrid architecture seeks to dynamically adapt to real-time network changes. This approach shows the promise for more dependable and energy-efficient routing solutions, which are essential for satisfying the changing needs of contemporary IoT networks, by directly addressing the interaction of real-time network dynamics and diverse device restrictions [87].

### 6.3.1 Particle Swarm Optimization (PSO) Principles and its Application in Networking

Particle Swarm Optimization (PSO) is a meta-heuristic optimization method inspired by nature that simulates the social behavior seen in fish schools and bird flocks. In many different fields, it is well known for its ease of use, efficacy, and efficiency in resolving difficult problems with optimization [88][89].

The following are the guiding concepts of PSO:

I. **Initialization:** Within the multi-dimensional search space, a swarm of particles is first created at random. A potential solution, like a potential routing path in an Internet of Things network, is represented by each particle. Every particle is given a random initial velocity and an initial position that corresponds to a particular routing path.

II. **Fitness Evaluation:** A predetermined fitness function is used to assess each particle's "fitness". This function usually takes into account several parameters at once for QoS-aware routing, including latency, energy usage, packet delivery ratio, and congestion in the network. A more desired option is indicated by a higher fitness value.

III. **Update Personal Best (pbest) and Global Best (gbest):** Each particle continuously monitors its own best position thus far during the optimization process; this is known as its personal best (pbest). At the same time, the global best position (gbest), which is the best solution found by any particle in the swarm thus far, is maintained by the entire swarm.

IV. **Velocity and Position Update:** Particles use a combination of their update their velocity and position. The update equations are:

$$\textbf{Velocity: } v_i(t+1) = \omega\, v_i(t) + c1\, r1\, (p_{best,i} - x_i(t)) + c2\, r2\, (g_{best} - x_i(t)) \qquad (6.1)$$

$$\textbf{Position: } x_i(t+1) = x_i(t) + v_i(t+1) \qquad (6.2)$$

Where $\omega$ is the inertia weight, which regulates how the particle's past velocity affects its present velocity. Acceleration coefficients c1 and c2 affect the pull in the direction of the particle's global best and personal best, respectively. The random values r1 and r2, which are usually in the range of 0 and 1, add stochasticity to the search procedure.

V. **Convergence:** The iterative procedure converges when a predetermined termination requirement is satisfied. A maximum number of iterations or the achievement of a desirable fitness value, which signifies the discovery of a reasonably effective solution, could serve as this criterion.

By taking into account several QoS measures at once, PSO can be used to improve routing paths in the context of IoT routing. This feature makes it possible to find almost ideal solutions in intricate, multi-objective network settings. PSO is especially well-suited for dynamic optimization problems where the optimal solution space is always changing because of its intrinsic iterative and adaptive nature, which is driven by both individual exploration influenced by personal best) and collective intelligence (directed by global best). PSO is a more flexible option for real-time IoT routing than static optimization techniques, which would necessitate a thorough recalculation with each modification in network conditions [90].

### 6.3.2 Graph Neural Networks (GNNs) Principles and their Relevance to Network Modeling

A type of deep learning architectures created especially to handle data in the form of graphs is represented by Graph Neural Networks (GNNs).The network topology in Internet of Things networks can be naturally expressed as a graph, with communication channels acting as edges and devices acting as nodes. By examining a complicated graph structure and the related characteristics of its nodes and edges, GNNs have the exceptional capacity to discover the best routing techniques [91] [92].

The working principles of GNNs are as follows:

I. **Graph Representation:** A graph G(V,E) is a formal representation of the Internet of Things network, with V representing the set of nodes (IoT devices) and E representing the set of edges (communication links). Every node and edge has a rich feature vector attached to it. Real-time data like device residual energy, link bandwidth, current link delay, and packet loss probability can all be included in these vectors.

II. **Message Passing and Aggregation:** A GNN's fundamental mechanism is an iterative message-passing system. Every node in the graph communicates with its immediate neighbors through messages, or information. Each node collects the information it has received after receiving messages from its neighbors. Summation, averaging, and more complex attention mechanisms are examples of common aggregation functions that enable the network to evaluate the relative relevance of various neighbors.

III. **Node Embedding:** A number of neural network layers are then traversed by the combined data for every node. Each node's updated "embeddings" are calculated by these layers. The local neighborhood qualities and the more general global network features important to the node's location and role in the graph are both well captured by these dense, low-dimensional numerical representations, known as embeddings.

IV. **Output Layer:** An output layer receives the final, learned embeddings. Determining routing scores for every potential next-hop node is the responsibility of this layer. To choose the routing path, the node with the greatest predicted score is then chosen as the packet's next hop.

V. **Training:** To increase the precision of their forecasts, GNNs undergo training. Reinforcement learning, in which rewards are granted based on the attainment of particular QoS metrics, or supervised learning, in which the best routing paths are supplied as labels, can be used for this training.

Because they can forecast the initial routing scores for each node by processing a complex IoT network graph, GNNs are essential to network routing. These scores, which are dynamically influenced by current network conditions, show the probability that a node is a member of an ideal routing path. GNNs offer a potent predictive routing mechanism because of their capacity to discover complex non-linear correlations in graph-structured data. By comprehending global network states and interdependencies, GNNs are able to infer optimal paths, as opposed to conventional routing algorithms that depend on local knowledge or pre-established rules. Instead of only responding to situations that are immediately adjacent, this enables the model to comprehend the network holistically and predict possible bottlenecks or ideal pathways across multiple hops, which is essential for proactive QoS management and preventing congestion before it emerges [93][94].

## 6.4 Proposed Hybrid Routing Mechanism

This section explores the chapter's main contribution by offering a thorough and in-depth description of the suggested PSO-GNN integrated architecture, its operational flow, and how it directly tackles the issues that have been discovered.

### 6.4.1 Detailed Description of the Integrated PSO-GNN Architecture:

In order to perform dynamic Quality of Service (QoS)-aware routing in heterogeneous IoT networks, a sophisticated combination of Particle Swarm Optimization (PSO) and Graph Neural Networks (GNNs) is represented by the suggested hybrid routing method. This framework intentionally draws on the beneficial qualities of both techniques: the predictive and adaptive capabilities of GNNs are paired with the optimization efficiency of PSO. In order to provide real-time insights into network statuses and traffic flows, the architecture enables the GNN to dynamically model the network topology. PSO is then used to optimize routing paths according to particular QoS requirements, like load balancing, throughput maximization, and delay minimization. In order to overcome the drawbacks of each technique when used separately, a hybrid model (GNN for prediction, PSO for optimization) was used as a strategic design choice. Although GNNs are excellent at identifying intricate patterns and forecasting outcomes, they can be computationally demanding for quick, real-time optimization. On the other hand, PSO is quite effective at optimization, but it does not have the "learning" ability to adjust to dynamically shifting network conditions without outside assistance. By utilizing each component's strengths and minimizing its shortcomings, its integration produces a strong collaborative impact that makes the solution more reliable and useful for dynamic IoT situations.

**6.4.2 How GNN Models the Network and Predicts Paths:** A key element in comprehending the dynamic Internet of Things network is the Graph Neural Network component. Real-time metrics including device energy levels, available link bandwidth, and current latency across connections are among the many node and link features that the GNN is built to learn from. To forecast the best routing routes, the GNN analyzes this graph-structured data using its message-passing and aggregation techniques. In particular, depending on the available QoS indicators, it generates anticipated edge weights that indicate how suitable certain routes are for routing.[1] A data-driven preliminary evaluation of possible routes based on current network conditions is provided by these projected scores, which show the probability that a specific node is a part of an ideal routing path [95].

### 6.4.3 How PSO Refines GNN Predictions Based on QoS Metrics

The optimization engine is Particle Swarm Optimization (PSO), which takes the GNN's initial routing path predictions and refines them to satisfy particular QoS goals. A well-crafted QoS-aware fitness function drives the refinement process. This feature incorporates a number of

QoS parameters, frequently weighted by application priorities, including latency, dependability, and energy efficiency. Reliability and low latency, for instance, may be given more weight in a mission-critical service. PSO refines the routing paths proposed by the GNN by iteratively exploring the solution space. Moving beyond local improvements to reach a globally superior solution, it measures and optimizes alternative paths based on global network properties such as overall load balancing and total energy usage across the network [96].

### 6.4.4 Feedback Loop and Real-Time Adaptation Mechanisms

The continuous feedback loop between PSO and GNN, which permits real-time adaptation and continual learning, is a crucial component of the suggested hybrid system. In the whole solution space, the PSO particles are not initialized at random. Rather, they are deliberately started with their initial placements determined by the predictions of the GNN. By guaranteeing that the optimization process starts with a superior, well-informed initial solution, convergence is greatly accelerated and the quality of the final routes is enhanced. These GNN-recommended routes are iteratively improved by PSO. The GNN then receives the improved, optimized routes from PSO. The GNN may learn from the globally optimum solutions identified by PSO thanks to this feedback, which acts as an updated training dataset. The GNN becomes increasingly intelligent and accurate with each optimization cycle as a result of this iterative process, which gradually improves the predicted accuracy over time. The system becomes a continuously learning and adapting intelligent agent as a result of this explicit feedback loop between PSO and GNN, which goes beyond simple sequential execution. By enabling the system to develop its routing intelligence over time rather than depending on static training, this self-improvement method is essential for preserving optimal performance in extremely dynamic and unpredictable IoT contexts where network conditions are continuously changing. Because of its quick reasoning capabilities, the GNN makes quick initial routing decisions during real-time network operation. PSO operates concurrently, continuously improving these choices to guarantee worldwide optimization and flexibility in response to sudden network fluctuations. Both rapid reactivity and continuous peak performance are guaranteed by this dual mechanism.

### 6.4.5 Algorithm for Dynamic QoS-Aware Routing with PSO and GNN

**A. Input**: A network graph with nodes V (devices) and edges E (communication links) is represented as G(V,E).

**B. Specified QoS Requirements:**

- Minimum necessary bandwidth ($Q_{bandwidth}$)
- Minimum reliability threshold ($Q_{reliability}$)
- Maximum permitted latency ($Q_{latency}$).
- The network's current traffic matrix.
- The highest possible number of PSO iterations (N).
- PSO's swarm size (S).

A. **Output:** Routing methods that are optimized to meet the given QoS criteria.

#### 6.4.5.1 Algorithm's Steps

I. **Step Network Initialization:**

- Create a graph G(V,E) that represents the current network topology.
- Gather up-to-date network state data, such as traffic trends, link capacity, and latency across all communication channels.

- Specify and set up the QoS measurements ($Q_{bandwidth}$, $Q_{reliability}$, $Q_{latency}$ and their thresholds.

**Step II. : GNN-Based Network Modeling:**

- To model the network dynamics, apply a Graph Neural Network (GNN) that has already been trained.
- Real-time node and edge features (such as traffic load, link bandwidth, and current latency) are sent into the GNN.
- The predicted edge weights, which indicate the appropriateness or acceptability of routes for routing based on the learnt QoS metrics, are the output from the GNN. To keep its predictions up to date, the GNN model is updated in real-time as network conditions change.

**Step III. Particle Swarm Initialization**

- Initialize a swarm of S particles.
- Assign random initial positions and velocities to particles in the solution space.
- Evaluate the fitness of each particle using a QoS- aware fitness function 6.3.

$$F(x) = w1 \cdot f_{latency} + w2 \cdot f_{bandwidth} + w3 \cdot f_{reliability} \qquad (6.3)$$

Where w1, w2, w3 are weights assigned to QoS metrics.

**Step IV. PSO Optimization**

1. **For each iteration t (1 to N)**: For each particle i in the swarm:

a. ***Update Particle Velocity:*** particle velocity is updated according to equation no. (6.1).

b. ***Update Particle Position*:** Updated particle position is calculated using equation no. (6.3).

c. ***Evaluate the fitness of the updated position.***

d. ***Update $p_{best}$ and $g_{best}$ based on fitness values.***

***Step V. Integration of PSO and GNN***

a. ***Feedback Loop:*** Use the GNN's predicted edge weights to guide the PSO search by biasing particle initialization and movement toward high-quality paths. Incorporate GNN predictions into the fitness function for real-time adjustment.

b. After each PSO iteration, update the network state in GNN to reflect changes due to routing decisions.

***Step VI. Termination and Routing Decision***

a. Terminate PSO after N iterations or if a convergence criterion is met.

b. Select the particle with the best fitness as the optimal routing solution.

c. Apply the selected paths to the network for data transmission.

***Step VII. Continuous Learning and Adaptation***

a. Periodically retrain the GNN model using updated network state data to improve prediction accuracy.

b. Adjust PSO parameters dynamically based on network size and complexity to ensure scalability.

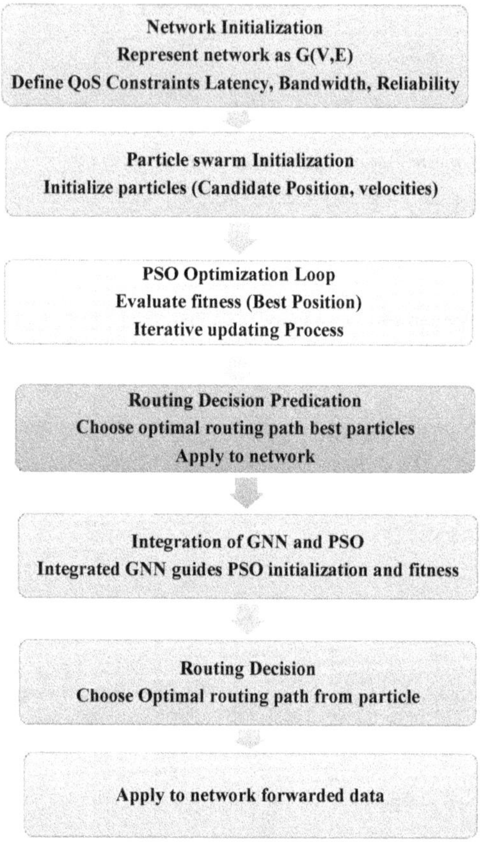


**Figure 6.1 Workflow of Dynamic Optimized QoS- Aware Routing**

### 6.4.6 Experimental Design and Simulation

The results given were obtained by carefully designing and implementing a comprehensive simulation environment in order to validate the suggested methodology. The network environment, traffic models, implementation specifics of the suggested algorithm, assessment metrics, and benchmarking techniques are among the elements of the simulation setup that are covered in this section.

#### 6.4.6.1 Simulation Environment

NS-3 (Network Simulator3), a well-known and often used simulation tool for network research, was used to carry out the simulations. In order to make algorithm implementation and GNN integration easier, Python scripts were integrated with NS-3. To accurately model various IoT devices, routers, and backbone links, a random graph generator was used to construct a heterogeneous network architecture. In order to fully test the scalability of the suggested method, the network size was adjusted between 100 and 500 nodes with different levels of connectivity. Each link was given a dependability factor between 0.8 and 1.0, latency between 1 ms and 50 ms, and bandwidth values between 1 Mbps and 10 Gbps, all of which were randomly assigned to represent real-world network situations.

#### 6.4.6.2 Traffic Model

The traffic model being considered recognized the existence of three types of application and all of them reflect a wide range of activities in an IoT network. The term types of application was given as follows:

- Characteristics of IoT device traffic that is low-bandwidth and latency-sensitive
- Video streaming, which is latency tolerant, high bandwidth-demanding.
- Extreme services where high-level reliability and strict low-latency requirements are needed.

To implement such variations in traffic behavior, Constant Bit Rate (CBR) traffic model as well as Poisson traffic model were used. The data flows were randomly generated so that the variations in the network conditions in real time were considered when evaluating the results, which in turn increased the robustness of the results.

#### 6.4.6.3 Implementation Details

**A. Graph Neural Network (GNN)**

In the application, Graph Neural Networks (GNNs) were applied to PyTorch Geometric, a deep-learning framework that specially supports graph-structured data. The three layer architecture was built, the input layer consisted of feature representation of nodes and edges such as traffic load, link delay, and bandwidth; the hidden layers incorporated a Graph Convolution operation with ReLU activation functions; the output represented output edge weight that was generated on the basis of an indicative value of the path worth routing based on QoS dimensions. The network was also pre-trained based on the available historical data about the network and then it was updated in real time during simulation to take into consideration the changing conditions that occurred on the network.

**B. Particle Swarm Optimization (PSO)**

The routing scheme used was fine-tuned with the help of the Particle Swarm Optimization (PSO). A total of 50 particles within PSO swarm were randomly initialized in terms of both position and velocity within the solution space. The fitness of each particle was determined via a fitness function that was being driven by QoS as given in equation no. (6.3).

**C. Integration of GNN and PSO**

The hybridization of Graph Neural Networks (GNN) and Particle Swarm Optimization (PSO) proved to be crucial to the overall framework. The GNN predictions gave PSO information concerning the initialization of the particles and to evaluate the candidate solutions, thus directing the search on fruitful paths.[1]After completing every single PSO iteration, the network state was modified and resubmitted to GNN to recalibrate, so a feedback loop of learning and adaptation was produced.

#### 6.4.6.3 Evaluation Metrics

The present methodology was measured on the basis of the following metrics.

I. **Latency:** Average time of end to end delay of data flow in the entire network.

II. **Utilization of Bandwidth**: Used bandwidth/available bandwidth.

III. **Packet Delivery Ratio (PDR):** Ratio of successfully delivered data packets sent to their destinations.

IV. **Computational Efficiency:** The time that the route optimization takes.

V. **Adaptability:** The amount of time required to redirect traffic in the event of breakdown within the network or when experiencing congestions.

##### 6.4.6.3.1 Benchmarking

The current study was a systematic review of a hybrid routing framework against three existing substitutes that were utilized to prove its superiority [1]:

A. **Heuristic-Based Routing:** The methodology proposed was expected to outperform the heuristic algorithms because it can efficiently adjust dynamically, which subsequently performs at a QoS compliance that is as much as 50 % higher [1].

B. **Standalone PSO:** By adding GNN, the expectation was that the hybrid model would achieve not only faster convergence and also greater reliability in comparison to PSO in isolation [1].

C. **Deep Learning Approaches:** The hybrid design was a trade-off between computational efficiency and QoS performance, thus being more realistic environmentally friendly as compared to its standalone deep-learning fancied counterparts.

The assessment was done through three different scenarios of simulation to provide detailed performance indicators:

I. ***Static Network Conditions:*** This scenario was used as a benchmark in determining primary efficiency and testing the infrastructure performance in idealized conditions.

II. ***Dynamic Scenarios:*** An inquiry on adaptability and robustness of the scenario was done by creating dynamic scenarios that would call upon the simulation in the link failures, congestion, and spikes in the traffic.

III. ***Scalability Tests:*** Increase of 100 then 500 nodes against time measured how the performance is scaled on the complexity of network, which gave scope about how appropriate the framework is on large scale settings.

### 6.4.7 Result Analysis

It has been shown that the combination of Particle Swarm Optimization (PSO) and Graph Neural Networks (GNN) has provided significant improvement in data routing in Internet of Things (IoT) networks especially in scenarios where Quality of Service (QoS) is paramount. Experiments have proved that this combination approach can provide better performance in terms of network, improves the flexibility of the network operations, and also promotes better scaling on large scale projects. The framework allows PSO to determine routes to maximize network efficiency, and at the same time reducing end-to-end delays and balancing data loads on the various route pathways because each GNN module has the ability to accurately map the network conditions. The joint solution, therefore, enhances the use of bandwidth and ensures the delivery of data that can be relied upon as the QoS covers aspects like reliability and latency among others in a clear manner. Moreover, the integration has some elements of computational efficiency due to the optimization features of PSO and shows quick adaption to dynamic conditions of the network. The results retrieved support the claim that the PSOGNN hybrid is an efficient, effective and QoS-sensitive routing mechanism. By binding the interaction between the individual strengths of the PSO and the GNN, the model would always yield a better performance in terms of computational cost, flexibility and QoS compliance, which is superior to both conventional and standalone solutions.

Table 6.1 summarizes the results of the proposed methodology compared to other commonly used heuristic procedures, standalone PSO, and deep-learning-only approaches as catalogued by various performance measures.

**Table 6.1: Comparison of Result between existing and proposed model**

| Metric | Proposed Approach | Heuristic Methods | Standalone PSO | Deep Learning Only |
|---|---|---|---|---|
| **Latency Reduction** | 30-40% improvement | Moderate | Limited | High (but slower) |
| **Bandwidth Utilization** | 25% better | Low | Moderate | Moderate |
| **Packet Delivery Ratio (PDR)** | >95% | <85% | 90-92% | ~94% |

| | | | | |
|---|---|---|---|---|
| **Computational Efficiency** | High | High | High | Moderate |
| **Adaptability** | Excellent | Limited | Moderate | Good |
| **Scalability** | Excellent | Moderate | Good | Good |

### 6.4.7.1 Discussion of Metrics

A. **Minimized Latency:** The hybrid architecture that is studied provides latency improvement of about 30-40 %, which is a considerable improvement over current techniques. This amount of end-to-end latency improvement is a necessity to real time IoT applications like remote surgery or autonomous car communication, where milliseconds of petition delay could lead to serious impacts.

B. **Bandwidth Utilization:** This model able to attain 25 percent increase in bandwidth usage. The efficiency that is provided by such increase makes it possible to have a high throughput of data and provide more bandwidth-intensive applications such as video streaming without causing congestion.

C. **Packet Delivery Ratio (PDR):** The design can deliver a high level of data delivery due to the value obtained exceeding 95 percent. This metric is authoritative in mission-critical services of IoT where data integrity and guaranteed delivery is a must; this metric would easily surpass heuristic methods that can achieve only below 85 percent PDRs.

D. **Computational Efficiency:** The routing decisions can be realized with negligible computational cost, therefore achieving fast execution without placing unnecessary demands on the limited resources of the devices or network nodes.

E. **Adaptability:** This is demonstrated by its ability to adjust traffic flows dynamically in real time to cope with the loss of a link, congested times or sudden surges of traffic and ensure that its service is available and its performance is optimized based upon a network whose conditions are inherently volatile.

F. **Scalability:** As experiential result shows, performance does not decrease significantly under the conditions of the increased number of nodes, being 100 or 500, and this feature points at the option to deploy it in large-scale and complex IoT systems with insignificant losses of efficiency or QoS compliance.

## 6.5 Summery

The proposed framework has helped to look at the predicament issues of present IoT networks, which are adaptive routing in dynamically changing topologies, effective utilization of resources and addressing non-homogenous Quality of Service (QoS) requirements, and clarify them completely. Through the prediction makings of the Graph Neural Networks (GNNs) and the optimization steps of the Particle Swarm Optimization (PSO) algorithm, the hybrid creation can apply effective and resistant rout pathways in the heterogeneous networks structure. The PSO module helps to optimize the routing paths toward globally optimized goals, and the GNN implementation makes time-specific, local decisions in terms of predicting the availability of routes towards the rapidly displayed change in the network. These two mechanisms make it possible to be both fast and globally optimized, which differentiates the suggested methodology with the traditional routing methods. Experimental outcomes show that there are huge performance gains, such as latency reduction, increased energy efficiency, and network performance, which support the success of the given architecture. Also, using the integration strategy, it is possible to scale to much larger IoT networks without sacrificing performance due to normal topology churning.

The fundamental routing issue is well covered, and, though related but still fundamental issues like security and privacy are mentioned as challenges, it is not explicitly covered in the solution which is proposed. This practical narrowness of scope is also an explicit direction of the future research.

The above work is published as research paper entitled "Dynamic Optimized QoS-Aware Routing using integration of Particle Swarm Optimization with Graph Neural Network" in International Journal for Research in Engineering Application & Management (IJREAM) ISSN : 2454-9150 Vol-11, Issue-02, May 2025.